JOHN TYLER

THE TRANSCENDENT AVENGER

DIPANJAN BHATTACHARJEE

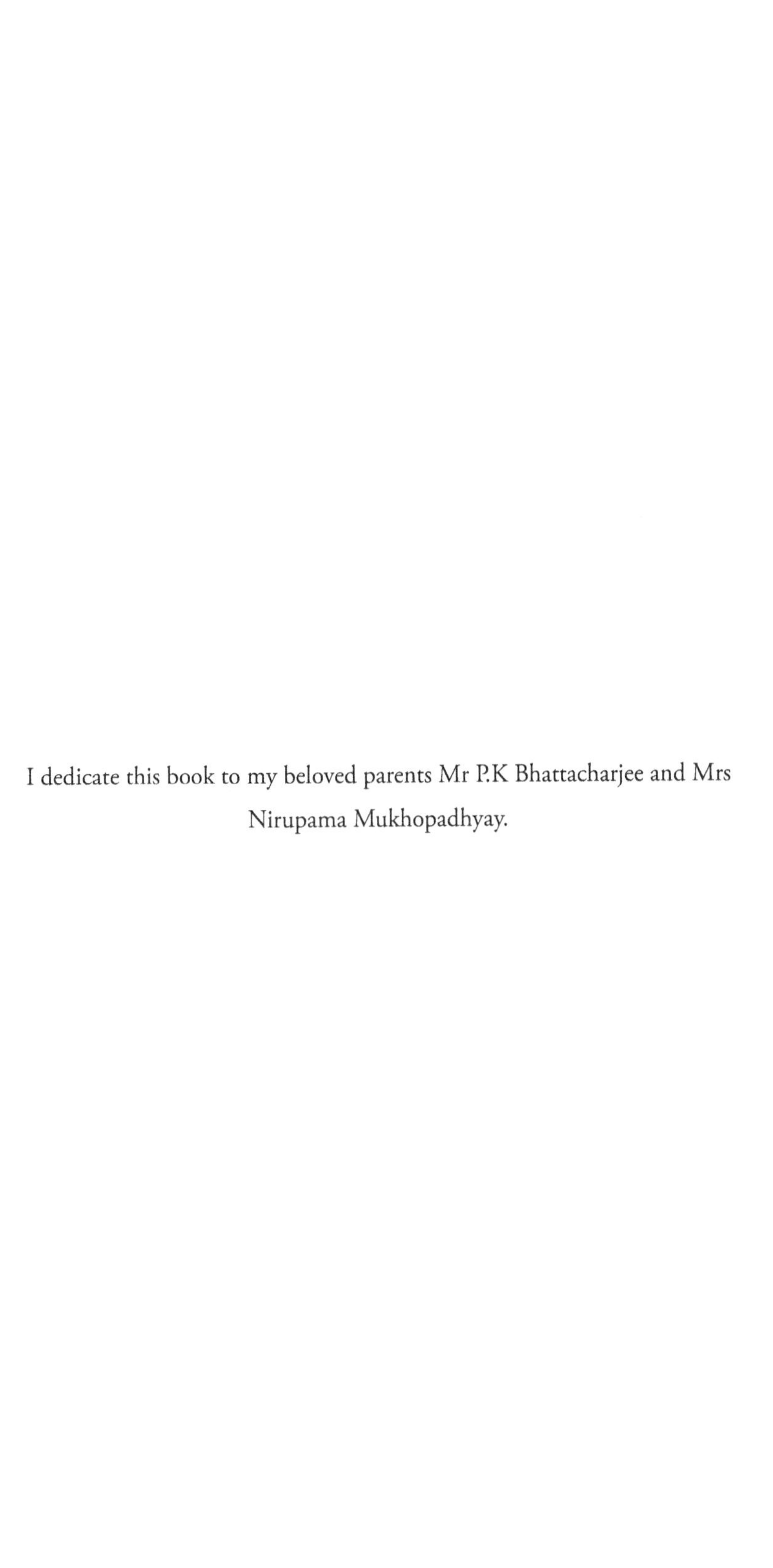

I dedicate this book to my beloved parents Mr P.K Bhattacharjee and Mrs Nirupama Mukhopadhyay.

Contents

Preface

Crime thrillers have been man's all-time favourite since ages. John Tyler is a novel where a very different and uncanny mind-set has been depicted all throughout. Wasted childhood often leads to a distorted personality and that in turn creates a human very different and eldritch from the common human race. John Tyler is a personality that is often termed as a psychopath in our modern world. He chooses a very different approach to penalize criminals who are often successful in escaping out from even the longest arms of law. Recreating exact scenes of crime as would be done by those potential criminals, he ensures a purgatory for them. In doing so, many innocent lives are sacrificed. The journey goes on through highs and lows and strange mazes with profound enigmas entwined in every turn of this novel. Ranging from uncanny happenings to adult whereabouts, and emotional surges to massive transformations, the entire book is a box of thrill and immense excitement.

Despite being an engineer by profession, I am an ardent preacher of literature. I am extremely attached with various forms of literature, especially poetry. I have written many more books as poetry collections, short story collections and also a full-fledged novel till date. This book is a very unique approach of mine in exploring the ultimate realm of literature. The entire novel is written is verse form with uniform quintets all throughout with a rhyme scheme of ABABB. I am quite anticipant that each and every reader of this book will appreciate the flow of the verses and the narrative that has been tactfully covered along with a uniform verse form. This will certainly make my readers get a glimpse of old English literature and also carry for them a typical scent of old pages from our high school libraries. I would certainly request each one of you to go through the entire story and also enjoy

Acknowledgements

I am forever thankful to my parents for their constant support and to the almighty God for his kind blessings bestowed upon me. This book has been inspired by a recent bengali movie named "Vinci Da".

Prologue

So how clenched be in thy hands,
The world of daring games?
Across distant seas and o'er the lands,
There is so much more in names.
And there is so much in mayhems.
Who's the force thou dost believe?
The driving arms since yore.
The arms that a million dreams weave,
And make each yearn for more.
And make each heart too sore.
Covetous desires allure death,
Dark nights breathe in hush.
They hanker and hanker for a breath,
But death keeps unleashing cuss.
And tis none but a profane blush.
Behold! The lone woman snapping thru' the dark,
Walks for home aft a day's work whole.
Ay! She's brave; she holds a divine spark,
But that's too confined to her oblivious soul.
And too oblivious to the evil's goal.
O the hound comes gushing behind,
Lustful vengeance thrives too sore.
A facinorous concourse with demonic minds,
Scuttle thru' the barren shore.
And grab her flesh with cussed amour.
Her bones fall frail to the wretched arms,

As she gasps for some more air.
The gory earth witness her wilted charms,
As she falls still o'er its helpless layer,
And bequeath to the world her tittle share.
There away few miles to the west,
Roads art bare beneath dark skies.
The solitary night o'er a thousand nests,
Hovers around with yawning eyes.
And hovers around in clean disguise.
Lo! Tis the fate of a hundred men,
Lying in slumber on paths untrod.
The rich man bibulous drives insane,
To slay off creations of the great God.
And so he pretends as a ruling Lord.
His wheels amuck o'er sleeping ones,
And crimson flood scurries down.
The count was ten or more perchance,
Their corpses lay still amid the town.
And I have seen the moon to frown.
Thrice this time but the good old God,
Could e'er but punish the evil sinner.
He savours wealth and with a sword,
Proclaims strong his ill demeanour.
And prances forth as a triumphant winner.
Now the morning with scarlet a face,
Smiles in glee o'er the awakened town.
The cops run haste; like a race,
And run a quest to chase 'em down,
And chase 'em but with an ireful frown.

PROLOGUE

Where art evidence? Who hast seen?
All voices hold no words to unveil.
The mortal town beneath moon sheen,
Had lain in slumber as a dead man's deal.
And had lain in slumber for a night to heal.
Let the files thus sleep in dust,
For longer years and longer eons.
No sinner could there be found on crust,
As the night stood witness alone.
And in hush stood the mourning dawn.
Then a melody ring for a while,
'Tis a call from the people's bank.
A sly offender sold his smile,
And stole the wealth in a sudden yank,
Leaving the visages pale and blank.
The befuddled cops scamper out,
And to the plunder'd bank they reach.
The camera's hold no voice or shout,
They saw the glimpses finer each.
There's no trace of a theft or breach.
What's but the story? The cops did ask,
Voiceless the manager bumbled shy.
Know not I o worthy Sir; no man in a mask
But stole the wealth. 'Twas not e'en a passer-by,
All by a click so traced nay guy.
Tricky! Very odd the heist was true,
And the cops were all stone amuck.
And thru' books they found no clue,
And left things all for the good old luck.

They're in words too bleakly stuck.

One for two and more such crimes,

Hurled terror thru' the gleaming towns.

The cops stood dumb thru' fiendish times,

Mere as silhouettes of silly clowns.

And their shameful visages hid in gowns.

John Tyler, a name not known,

Now shalt rein my tale in verse.

Sinful ones that in mirth had grown,

Now must face the wands too worse,

And must bewail the tryst with curse.

1. FIRST RENDEZVOUS

Poor Jerry by the dales of north,
An artist true to; but lone himself.
No man e'er did feel his worth,
No man e'er did seek his help,
Yet days he counted in his delf.
Visages aplenty he made each day,
For; the art itself serv'd him joy.
Big brown faces to the ones in grey,
He play'd all day with a room of toys.
They're mannequins but for him; his begotten boys.
One lone eve off all the tasks,
Poor Jerry was walking dales.
A zephyr came soft with the falling dusk,
And kiss'd him love o'er the barren vales,
'Twas a solitary soldier of the retreating gales.
Thither on the darkly muffled benches,
A solitary shadow was perching all at ease.
The fizzog uncanny masquerading the wenches,
Awaited as if for the sun too wilt o'er the trees,
And sat too still to the ruffling evening breeze.
Curious Jerry gazed a while and longer perhaps,

Who's the man perching sans a goal?
Or a goal perchance he knows; brumous snaps
For a moment scared his timid soul,
Is he then a pilferer who's here for the King's amber bowl?
Short and silent to the brook and saw he then,
The man's someway in midst decades four.
Stout health and a broader chin,
Lost eyes somewhere down the no man's shore.
Perhaps afar to some treasure door.

JERRY:

"Lo thou! What business dost thou hold?
Wherefore art thou hither perching in hush?
Art thou a pilferer on a sinful quest for gold?
Dubious I shalt ne'er sate to thy innocent blush;
Thou must in heart possess a nefarious purpose."
O those bright pair of eyes; amber hued,
Gazed at the silly folk blabbering in delight.

JOHN TYLER:

"Art thou Jerry; the artist whose work ain't subdued?
But oft less spoken of amid the broad daylight.
I pity thou o skilful soul! I commiserate thy plight."
The words from a strange one cockled his bare head,
"O how on the good old land must he know my skin?"
The man spoke! "Aghast art thou? I'm still unsaid,
The tale awaits a thousand words and many a din,

The edge holds gold and a wealthy win."
Bemused a blink! Jerry quaffed the spit inside,
His queasy arms shook a while few words he said.

JERRY:

"Who art thou o man? This poor soul ne'er had a guide,
Alone the world and all good dreams to my brains were fed,
For; my arms and fingers with my soul forever stayed."

JOHN TYLER:

"Know not I; what odds touched thee?
Wherefore art thy skill ne'er so well preserved?
No man hath e'er entrusted upon thy true beauty,
All for wealth but all for sinners their choices served,
And for the evil their hearts art so well reserved.

JOHN TYLER:

Fear not mate! John must for certain pander thy dreams,
Thy skills to this world of justice shalt be well framed.
Sinful ogres to the dark dungeons but weep and scream,
And for the sins for a longer life they must be ashamed,
And o'er years midst bleak old cells their souls shalt be tamed."
O for a while those words uncanny settled afar,
Solitary stood in baffled an hour his feet on earth.
Or no earth but o'er amid the scattered stars,
Swirling head kept twirling wider thru' the garth.

Poor Jerry now in remorse cuss'd his birth.

JERRY:

"Who art thou? What seek'st thou? O know not I,
Unveil to me thy countenance and thy worthy race.
What business dost thou hold? Let me and my-
Soul; breathe solitude. I'm gay in my own chase,
Of creating mannequins and breathing in their face.

JOHN TYLER:

"Offer me a minute boy! Let me speak a while,
I'm not a macabre man on earth but a noble one indeed.
Hear my name; 'tis John Tyler and now thou must smile,
Thy dormant art shalt soar the skies and slay off lust and greed,
And with thy tender arms again nurture the torpid seed.

JOHN TYLER:

Hither hold this picture bright; make a fizzog so neat,
And I shalt to you a fortune pay and wealth shalt kiss thee deep.
An artist art thou o noble soul; let treasures adorn thy feet,
And enthrone thy timid soul that's still in graves asleep.
The mournful days art lost forever, no longer shalt thou weep."
Poor Jerry had ne'er in life a fortune earned at once,
His art mourned lone amid the realm of enclosed walls.
Bleak hues to him now served another tinselled chance,
And he must sate the Tyler man; ere the darkness falls.

Tis perchance can serve to him a bunch of abundant calls.

2. JERRY'S REMORSE

Two short days and then he's hands were holding the little face,
'Twas of Mike; the roguish soul, who lived in north down town,
Fifty one a damsel bled and ne'er returned to race,
'Twas a joy to the infernal soul as he snapped thru' gowns,
No cop could e'er with crude evidence grab him in this town.
Ten thousand dollars put forth! Jerry danced too gay,
His little art that seldom smiled feted a worthful joy.
And off in winds the Tyler man had no words to say,
He seemed quite elated too and thus the eldritch boy,
Thought Jerry, had no words to praise his little toy.
Few hours scurried in haste; the news read aloud,
"Vianca Burns was dead and raped brute too hard."
The footage unleashed 'twas Mike the raper and that he's proud,
And grimaced to the camera lens; though he's unheard,
'Twas bleak a night the day before; a Vianca had no guard.
Jerry stood high and wept aloud; "what sin I've done!
Is that Tyler; the holy soul and is that what I made?
O Jesus! Bless me mercy; 'twas ne'er for mundane fun,
'Twas for a purpose, Tyler said and quite a time he said,
'Twas to purge the sinful men with slight a phoney dread."
There he stood, John Tyler! His smile was too beguiling,

JOHN TYLER:

"Look good mate! And that's old Mike being dragged into the cell.
And that's for thou! Thy noble work," his face still too smiling,
One the sinner, is knocked off far; and he must taste sweet hell,
But stop not us until 'em all! Hear the Godly bell."
Perceived! Yet my noble heart moans for that girl,
Innocent was her chaste soul; ne'er to sin she bowed.
For what sin she'd been punished? Her little pair of pearls,
Gaze lifeless at the bare sky; her carcass in hush echoed,
The voice of her tormented soul with agony was bestowed.

3. TRICKY TYLER

JOHN TYLER:

Jerry o dear noble heart! Quoth the Tyler man,
When battles play'd 'tween regal knights,
And battles play'd with fiendish clans,
For many a day and umpteen nights,
Tittle lives art sacrificed; yet the ends smile bright.

JOHN TYLER:

Just for a moment think'st thou;
Had not Mike been out-winged the way,
And had he well feted his sins too now,
A hundred Viancas each a day,
Must've lost their voice to say.

JOHN TYLER:

Once a girl and her valiant life; quoth he,
And Mike would be but shackled fore'er;
Into the dungeons. The bleak old sea-
Shalt purge him off his sinful layers.
Ay! And thus we shalt baptise the demonic airs.

JOHN TYLER:

And now thou must this image behold'st,
For; Tis the Dover! The "Pavement Slayer".
And if perchance he's left to nest,
Many a man shalt sleep fore'er.
With clamorous groans; soaring the air.
Jerry; the artist bemoaned a while,
And his soul that's baffled; mourned anguish.
There's but another thought and a smile,
Of rising dreams and a triumphant wish.
His divine skills now thru' the world vanquish.
His grinning lips to the daffy Tyler,
As herald to another world class art,
Came joyful with a tranquil smiler,
"O Jerry! So off to the winds I depart,
And aft a day shalt return to my rosy styler."
The moon was tranquil in the sky,
And the beams too calmly descending.
Jerry: the artist with a raring eye,
Worked all night with scissors bending,
And countless hours in work he's spending.
Whole long night with the crescent moon,
Stood witness to his aweary toil.
Dover's visage was bright too soon,
A visage too vibrant in turmoil.
And by the day 'twas draped in a foil.
The morn kept warm with the sun o'er head,

And Jerry's engrossed to contemplate.
The laws of goodness to him still said,
Each sinner must face his condign fate,
And that must come with a precise date.

JOHN TYLER:

Hola Jerry! This' Tyler here; wake up,
The clock runs faster than worthy time.
And so must we! Thy doors art closed; dup!
Dup 'em open to the jocund moon; feel the rhyme,
Tis a canoe this night; swaying as a dulcet chime.

JOHN TYLER:

And now no more John Tyler speaks,
Tis none but Dover for business leaves.
Rest a while; with these lifeless geeks,
And I must assure that Dover heaves,
And be plunged to the hell he ne'er believes.
And oblivious to the beaming canoe,
Jerry was lost in a savouring slumber.
The little moon but in silence saw,
The other side where a decade number,
On pavements slept o'er a barren lumber.
'Neath wheels amuck miming Dover,
Tyler's vehicle squelch'd 'em all.
They were ten and all were woodland rovers,
And they slept in peace beneath moon-fall.

Quite too oblivious of Thanato's call.
The pavement saw more blood and flesh,
Scattered like those slaughter'd beings.
Gory the earth too mourned disgrace,
For, for her children; sweet those things,
Whose life's more of a bird sans wings.
The early dawn saw corpses galore,
They had lain all night but for a glance.
As with the sun few men from the shore,
As passer-by there came perchance;
And all they beheld was a gory countenance.
They scuttled berserk but for the cops,
Cuz only the cops must intervene.
Sad the morning with bleak raindrops,
Washed the gore and off the scene,
And onto the moors that's no longer green.
The cops did come and saw the zone,
And thru' the lens they saw a face.
'Twas the same old Dover alone,
And his vehicle scurried the deadly race,
Slaying the rovers as a grave disgrace!

DOVER:

"O know not I whose car went feral,
I was but off a hundred miles; quoth the Dover.
Trust me! I just deal in murals,
And no envy o'er the hapless rovers,
Pity on 'em! But this time 'twas not the Dover."

COPS:

"Close thy words! Speak not thee,
Thy phoney voice must ne'er us sate.
The footage saw we; all of we,
And that too lucid ruined thy fate.
Now come with us; O Dover the Great!"
The cops did drag him off his floor,
And plunged him into the ebony clink.
Swampy walls and an iron door,
And just some water to eat and drink.
And hourly lashings that barred him blink.
The city news of all the tales read aloud,
And 'twas Jerry who's learned heart knew it all,
The truth! 'Twas not Dover that drove o'er the sleepy crowd,
'Twas Tyler whose voice mimed Thanato's call.
And thus the truth as complicity echoed his hall.
The barren pavement drenched cerise,
Lay entwined in a melancholic reminiscence.
Higher among the clouds and skies,
There's sorrow and there's an essence-
Of anguish; auguring an outburst of tempestuous vehemence.
And there in hush for hours two,
Stood Jerry brooding deeper than e'er.
He's too a comrade or a treasonous beau!
And that is the truth. His wider share,
Hast slayed 'em all. O so venomous is the air.
His withered soul no more can word,

And these walls seem like a cage.
And his bereft soul, like a wounded bird,
Mourns in agony midst outrage.
He's but a sinner transformed from an exalted sage.
The door opened with a wide moonlight,
Jerry's aweary face as a wilted flower in a stormy garth,
Gave no worth to Tyler who's now glinting bright,
No remorse! All sins of this ginormous earth,
Shalt but ne'er decrease Mr Tyler's foaming mirth.

JOHN TYLER:

"Ain't thou gay o dear mate? Cheer the skies,
'Tis another sinful traitor who's lashed to death.
It calls for a celebration! Wherefore thine eyes
Teary at this gleeful hour? Art thou losing faith?
Thou art an artist with the most savoured breath."

JERRY:

"Abandon mine home! Get straight to thine way,
Thou art the disciple of insanity profound.
Leave me to my fate! I'm strangling thru' the day,
Thy voice stabs me like a clamorous sound,
Spare me o man or feed my corpse to a hungry hound."

JOHN TYLER:

"Slack a while o little man! Breathe a moment's air,

Know not thou what thither awaits.
Hold me closer and be my pair,
And I shalt embellish thy wilted fate.
And a day thou must reign as Jerry: The Great!

JOHN TYLER:

But if perchance thou to me refuse,
And work not to my gestures long.
I shalt to the cops produce,
All evidences that shalt stand too strong,
And in e'ery way prove thou wrong."

JERRY:

"What vengeance dost thou seek'st this day?
Wherefore to me thou hurl thine ire?
Let me breathe; let my soul not wither away,
Or burn alive in vengeful fires.
And drown each day in penitent mires.

JERRY:

This man's an artist with echt demeanour,
And truthful has my business been.
Tis noble a bourgeoisie and ne'er a sinner,
And ne'er for wealth my heart was keen.
And carried till day an artless sheen.

JERRY:

Tis remorseful wherefore by the brook,
That bleak evening cussed my day.
For; poor Jerry ne'er learned to rook,
And hither mine art hath ta'en away,
Innocent souls; their hearts still yearn to say."
Jerry's words were much bereavement,
Perching amid those bare woodlands.
Jerry stood like a horse on rent,
Doomed to scurry o'er tepid sands.
And scuttle all day with fettered hands.
Tyler spoke now; more soft than ere,
His voice was now too calm and beguiling.

JOHN TYLER:

What worth o' dear has kissed thy share?
For priceless an art that's evermore smiling.
This brute old world shalt break thy piling.

JOHN TYLER:

And I must proffer a deal too rewarding,
Cuz thine arms deserve true gold.
Wherefore then with an iron swording,
Stab'st thou thy own sweet mould
And break 'em clay ere they're sold?
Jerry arose too deep and pondering,

His eyes were as still as they could be.
His thoughts unfettered; wildly meandering,
Swam hard thru' the delirious sea,
And he thought; my art is worthful and isn't for free.

4. GERALD'S PURGATORY

JOHN TYLER:

Oh behold dear mate! 'Tis Gerald, the killer,
And now another wicket must fall.
He's name is adorned with many a thriller,
Yet does good deeds o'er phoney calls,
And stabs good men behind the palls.

JOHN TYLER:

He allures damsels to fete sweet nights,
And bask in flames of concupiscence.
Yet with the sun and the morning bright,
The erstwhile night turns a paltry reminiscence.
And the sly Gerald cloaks back in innocence.

JOHN TYLER:

Two score damsels hath fallen prey,
And lost fore'er their chaste good souls.
They mourn for life; perhaps each day,

And in anguish weep with a cruddy whole;
Their eyes too bleak with smudgy kohl.

JOHN TYLER:

Three decade men he'd slayed at ease,
And still walks in quest for many more.
With noble words as a susurrus breeze,
He tempts them all to his deuced door.
And buries their corpses 'neath bare shores.

JOHN TYLER:

A million pounds in his bank safe locks,
Lie well hued in a sinful blood.
Yet to him they serve great stocks,
And keep him happy amid red floods.
He's Gerald; a man too sly as the ebony birds.

JOHN TYLER:

Now this game to thy good choice,
And I must wait for a word from thou.
Thou must snub the chaffy voice,
And indulge thyself; in business now.
Take an oath and make a vow.

JERRY:

Three days and thy job is done,
Jerry voiced to Tyler; firm.
His voice depicted vehement acumen;
And there's a shine in his charm,
And a movement in his astir arms.
Two days and yet two longer nights,
Tyler ne'er bothered the man of art.
Jerry for a day quested insights,
And couldn't really find a part,
That shalt serve him a bash to depart.
The second morn plunged him job,
And into the task of Gerald's skin.
And Gerald's face in a perfect robe,
Now painted his lips with a cagy grin,
And a joy to work but win.
By the night the fizzog smiled,
As if Gerald is perching there.
He saw thru' the bench where moulds were piled,
And found a mould that mimed a pair,
To well restore his departed share.
The brighter morn with the descending morrow,
Will perhaps bring some expectant story.
And some goodness void of sorrow,
Shalt be a part of the morning glory.
For no actions hence; Jerry must e'er be sorry.
The brook was calm with ripples serene,
As Jerry walked o'er the silent dale.
The susurrus breeze from the distant green,
Augured bliss amid e'ery wail

That dwelled in him. It's time for a new sail.

JOHN TYLER:

Hola friend! Tis Tyler hither again,
Lend me thy noble arms; clasp it; hold it firm.
'Tis the gift well merited from an insane
Soul to thee. 'Tis a sequin ring with magical charms,
And shalt strengthen thy timid arms.
Jerry had no words to speak or to utter a voice,
He has perhaps found a road to the awaited freedom.
Ne'er more shalt he slave; sans his noble choice,
And walk miles afar from this barmy thraldom.
But for now he smiled and greeted the dippy worm.

JOHN TYLER:

Wow! He said! 'Tis perfect and so cool,
No wonder thou art an artist worth the world.
Thy skills proclaim a whole school,
And yearn to soar higher than the clouds unfurled.
Thou deserve indeed the King's castle of gold.

JOHN TYLER:

Swear I; to thee o man! A day shalt knock thy door,
The world shalt kiss thy tinselled arms,
And thou shalt quoth; "No More!"
Each a soul must seek thy charms,

And a blessing for life from thy divine arms.

JERRY:

Oh! I'm flattered but thou must now for business go,
A mount of tasks waits for thee.
Plunge the churl into the dark; let ne'er the deuced crow,
E'er return to this mortal garth to litter within the sea.
Set him free from cussed desires! O Tyler! Set him free.
Tyler felt a gust of joy as Jerry spoke his voice,
There's another holy man whom Tyler can praise.
He left in glee to rein his choice,
And to triumph his divine chase.
'Tis but for him; another invigorating maze.
'Twas the first night and Gerald was asleep,
Oblivious to the noble foe who awaits in hush.
The night was dark than e'er it was; so deep
And dense and fuming. The moon carried blush
But 'twas ephemeral. The silence was harsh.
John Tyler walked streets till an ebony nook,
A mendicant perched or perhaps in dreams.
Tyler stood for a little while like a duke,
Awaiting the prey in his fancy whims.
The pauper was thoroughly drenched in silver moonbeams.
And an axe went higher and yet higher,
And came back harsh to chop the man; too brute!
Gory the pavement seemed; as cerise mire,
The moon in melancholy cloaked its resplendent beaut,
And behind the nebules stayed conceal'd from the harrowing hoot.

The roads were barren beneath the tacit night sky,
The mourning stars shower'd their anguish'd raindrops.
Tyler's visage was covert and too sly,
And his feet scurried in haste tampering o'er the crops,
Down the fields and woodlands until the brook; he stops.
He's cloaked well within Gerald's countenance,
And all the lenses read it as he sought.
The bleak next morn stood hushed as if in trance,
And the corpse lay gory o'er the pavement plot.
'Twas as smooth as John Tyler thought.
Gerald was dragged and hurled into the dark,
The prison was befouled with filth piled for eons.
He yelled for truth and claimed; tis not his work,
But no ear hence desired to hear his moans,
And was sentenced to a lifetime's lashing and groans.
The proud Tyler returned to the cottage by the river,
Jerry though was nowhere traced, saw he;
Baffled he waited for hours like a jaded beaver,
But all in vain. No wind could speak of Jerry,
This strained Tyler's nerves like a forbidden cherry.

5. THE CONFESSION

There's a knock on the metallic door quite hard,
The sergeant flung it wide to behold a face;
Not quite known as if adorned in fard,
Standing hushed with eyes too scared of a chase,
Or perhaps too scandalous of disgrace.
He held a chip that he hurled forth in haste,
And scampered into the folds of thin air.
The sergeant scurried behind howling in behest,
The man was off in blinks; as a fuming atmosphere,
Leaving behind a chip as his only share.
Blue inked chip uncanny; perhaps some secrets within,
The sergeant play'd it on to hear a fretful voice.

UNKNOWN VOICE:

"To thou o worthy man! Hither a catch to win,
Tis guilt that makes me talk; tis my noble choice
To unveil myself. Tis not just an otiose noise.

UNKNOWN VOICE:

Hear me till the shore; hear until I stop,
There's a lot to speak; a lot to reveal.
I'm the one behind! I've ruined all verdant crops

From the fecund wombs. 'Twas a gory deal,
And I've travelled miles on those sinful wheels.

UNKNOWN VOICE:

My greetings to thee o Lord! John Tyler is my name,
And I've done the jobs the cops could ne'er do.
Sinners would slay more lives and savour their fiendish games,
And the credulous cops shalt watch; bare lands 'neath the blue.
And scurry for no cause and scurry with no clue.

UNKNOWN VOICE:

Fair deals ne'er seek justice; they're fair as they are,
But the deals of greed are ne'er fair on this earth.
Rover, Mike, Gerald and many more gleaming stars,
Committed sins galore; perhaps right from birth,
And plunged a hundred lives into noxious garths.

UNKNOWN VOICE:

What sin hast mine arms committed?
Recreating screens of gory happenings.
Miming the sinners alone; miming the mannequins of dread,
Proffering 'em a life so just for sinister beings,
And pushing 'em abysmally into the trench of stings.

UNKNOWN VOICE:

This voice holds truth and pride, and holds an eternal joy,
But there's remorse too and that's wherefore I talk.
Crime has ceaseless miles and I'm still tittle a boy,
Bereft too I am for many an innocent lives; I can't walk,
Can't sleep, can't breathe! My soul feels caged in a lock.

UNKNOWN VOICE:

And if perchance find'st thou a visage as mine,
Apprehend me whole! I shalt ne'er rebel.
I must reconcile cuz I've lost my will to shine,
This life seems bleak as hell,
And I'm drowning yet no desire to rise and sail."
The sergeant stood in awe! No words to speak,
His ears and mind lost tracks as a baffled soul.
What next? Thought he in hush! He felt frail and weak,
But duty must rein hours and duty must be the goal,
The man must be pinched soon in his breathing whole.
Befuddled Mr Stevens called for the troops,
And hurried in haste to the long boardroom.
He play'd the clip a couple of loops,
And sought a clue amid the fumes.
Tis now a case to guess or assume.
The morning enfolded the yawning world,
Tyler waited longer than one whole night.
Jerry ne'er but returned for the crate of gold,
Tyler promised to ameliorate his plight.
He has found another world of glee and delight.
Grave remorse kept nestling for days,

And perched firmly within his chaste heart.
Poor Jerry couldn't bury the disgrace,
That makes him a sinner too for his art,
And thus 'tis time for an artist to depart.
Tyler strolled by the tranquil brook,
And felt a hush that slayed his soul.
The world seemed drowsy thru ' e'ery nook,
And no man perhaps now holds a goal,
This (he thought) is a herald to a tempest foul.
Just a moment of placid air,
And then a storm came gushing by.
The clouds turn'd dark with frowning layers,
And ireful seemed the evening sky.
Purgatory (he felt) is now too nigh.
Seething troops were on every side,
They enfolded each road that's meant to tread.

COP TROOPS:

Reconcile o noble man! There's no cave to hide,
Plan not scatting! Surrender instead,
We shalt ensure thy shelter and bread.

POLICEMEN:

Glad art we! Indeed! Cuz thou confess'd,
Thy truth must decrease thy purgatory,
Promise I; Thou art a soul too blest,
With a mind that deserves to breathe free,

And for the crimes I must salute to thee.
Their noble words couldn't but reach his mind,
He plann'd a way to escape.
And jumped sooner into the river behind,
And swam yet faster with all his shape,
To kiss the yonder oval cape.

SERGEANT MR STEVENS:

"Fire!" Order'd the sergeant soon,
"Let his demise serve us triumphant delight.
There're yon skies and there's the moon,
Let 'em all hear his moans thru' the night.
He's a sinner and thus his plight.
The dark night crept faster than ere,
And Tyler's corpse was found nowhere.
They sought thru' the brook and e'ery layer,
But nothing haptic could sate 'em there,
Yet the sergeant quested long and fair.
Two days passed in cyphers and noughts,
And an evening came as a twisted tale.
By a lake lost in a caboodle of thoughts,
The sergeant traced a corpse by the dale,
Decayed perhaps; reeking with the gale.
This end had lain untrod for years aplenty,
Bare moorlands enfolded with thickets galore.
The lake streamed in hush of a solitary beauty,
Of swamps and marshes and sycamore.
Mr Stevens grew baffled with a mind that's huffy and sore.

There he found a tan leather bag,
Or rather a wallet with pence few pounds.
The defunct man was clad awful; in a tittle rag,
Torn at places by perhaps the woodland hounds.
This place is overly tranquil sans mundane sounds.
Jerry Thomson read the name on a card,
His identity is quite unfamiliar to his eyes.
All at once he beheld a can of fard,
And a prosthetic mannequin to his surprise.
"This man certainly has been befooling in disguise."
The sergeant for a moment reminisced,
And walked hind thru' the boulevard of memories,
The chip man at his door ne'er looked a slayer or a heist,
But a man with a scent of some leery stories,
Of murders and crimes and libellous glories.
He quested thru' crates of obscure memories,
And found but a visage li'l familiar though.
Gosh! 'Twas Tyler but there's an enigma in all these stories,
And mustn't I in hush just let it grow,
And to me these baffling fables show.
If he's Tyler who himself to my door show'd up;
And offered the chip where he confess'd.
Wherefore but he then from his cage broke up;
And jumped amuck into the fluvial chest?
The sergeant sensed some grave unrest.
As for a while he reminisced in hush,
His keen eyes beheld the mannequin lie,
'Twas bedraggled by the laky backwash,
Yet lucid to comprehend beneath the eve sky,

Jesus! Tis Tyler too; he couldn't trust his own bare eye.

SERGEANT MR STEVENS:

Conspiracy! Something leery is unfurling,
And I as a fool stand tacit to these games."
He felt the gushing storms now swirling;
And ruffling his bare face with covert mayhems.
Tyler and Jerry! Jerry and Tyler! Two elusive names.
The mannequin was sent off in a while,
And the corpse for autopsy was ta'en away.
Mr Stevens stood a dupe and gazed thru' the mile,
Threads of mystery got entwined with each passing day,
And as a nit he stands sans much to say.
The man who walked few days ere to his apartment door,
Is the one as a corpse who lied by the bare dale.
Suicide? Murder? What holds truth? He needs to learn more,
He needs to fetch the elixir now from the deadly whale,
And quaff it whole all at once o'er this solitary vale.
The man was well attired within the mannequin,
And thus the visage apart than on his card.
Purpose thrived well to protect or to ruin,
But his countenance so clothed an aroma of fard,
And that has been uncanny and terribly absurd.
But to him all at once a tale unveil'd its face,
Innocence squalled its existence; o'er his defunct countenance.
Thirty years of learning amid this arduous rat-race,
And thus the curtains hung astride unleashing a glance
Of truth; of crude reality and of a tale of impellent assistance.

And as an aid to the baffled mind and soul,
Came; the reports from the forensics.
The corpse and Tyler were ne'er same but perhaps with goals,
Similar, as Jerry's an artist of prosthetics,
And Tyler's a player with guiles and tricks.
So 'twas a story coming out from obscure skies,
And as a lucid moon now to him; gleamed bright.
Jerry was a man with skills; brimming his eyes,
And his art could've created brighter days amid bleak nights;
And its glorious glimpses must've allured many an eyesight.
All done and dusted now; the case nears the line,
Just the corpse of John Tyler is still in disguise,
Or perhaps devour'd by the gluttonous beasts divine,
The sergeant thought a while; was that delusions that kiss'd his eyes?
Or the ravening phantom's sorcerous game of dice?
The sergeant was a bard of whims ere the cop of fame,
And thus to thoughts and introspection he's oft reconciled.
The case was closed but yet to him the pair of swaggering names,
Created surges of ceaseless wonder and oft in dreams they smiled,
And smiled too the mannequins peeping from the wild.
The fragrance of the reeking lakes and the can of fard,
And the bleak skies of despondence; was all for him enwrapped.
The sergeant with his broken quill was now a moonstruck bard,
His pen and gun thru' scurrying hours were queerly swapped,
And his life on gothic roads; were like a delusion; mapped.
Few more lines we found him write,
Few more poems on pages he wrote.
And a stringent cop 'neath broad daylight,
Is now a bard with poetic quotes,

His river changed and so his boat.
"Two souls met beyond yon skies,
Where no man can e'er dwell.
Their bare souls now sans smooth disguise,
Landed within the sands of hell,
With diverse stories with each to tell.
'Tis remorse that drove an artist's mind,
'Tis remorse that purged his blemishes all.
And till another birth he finds,
It shalt serve him the strongest call,
And ne'er ever shalt let him fall.
Tyler must though to the world return,
With vengeance devouring his wandering soul.
Unfinished a life still makes him burn,
And chase a quest for his vengeful goals.
Perhaps; another name to endorse his role."

6. THE RETURN

Guanian Hills

Two years after Tyler's death

Beethoven's strings were heard; frail though,
From yonder pastures; miles to north.
The lands went skies and then too low,
Scraggy visage of the barren earth,
Sought perhaps for a plethoric garth.
Hither down-lands by the green wood lush,
A little cottage was seen by none.
The glimpses of the dayspring rush,
Enshrouded the cottage beneath the sun,
As there were none but only one.
Conical face and a broader chest,
The man was heard to speak no word.
Ne'er a voice of firm behest,
Thence in winds were ever heard,
O pity I feel for the ludic birds.
Graceful skies with azure sheets,
As duvets swayed in the morning breeze,
And hovered o'er the fields of wheat;

Bathed golden amid a thousand trees;
Dancing bibulous to the westerlys.
Oblivious a man to the eternal beaut,
Perched in hush with a pistol black.
Tempestuous storms were far; too brute;
And flooded his mind with the memory's stack;
Raffishly placed on subtle racks.
Two long years and the world changed shades,
A sphere indeed but a kaleidoscope.
Lands change shapes; the moon too fades,
And smiles back whole with a bowl of hope,
And stars lay twinkling as twisted ropes.
Of new work charts and new deals bright,
And crimes perhaps but fruitful ones.
There in the woods in dark bleak nights,
A man sits weaving dreams in trance,
Perhaps he seeks a fairer chance.
He's reading by the table at a wispy nook,
A little lanthorn illumes too frail.
A diary seems a bedraggled book,
Yet priceless to this orphic male,
Cuz it holds in pages John Tyler's tale.
John Tyler! A chapter closed two years before,
And no trace could ever be proven true.
All cops did hunt but 'neath sycamores,
Thus left forlorn like a defeated crew,
And riveted eyes on cases anew.
A man was seen not oft but a day,
Strolling by the northern dale.

They're tribes for years; nomads they say,
And hunt for moles thru' chartreuse vales,
And hunt mid morns in tepid gales.
They saw him walk and breathe good air,
And maunder softly with the breeze,
With dubious a visage like an old betrayer.
They saw him talk to the woodland trees,
And smile insane at the swimming geese.
Dark tan cloak was draped on skin,
Eyes were hazel as sleep depriv'd.
Bones look'd frail yet a balmy grin,
Clad his lips though too contriv'd,
As a man from ashes aft years; reviv'd.

7. THE TRYST

Dora lived bleakly by the northern brook,
Entwined around the woodlands green.
In the village of tribes with a faery look,
She hued in gold sparkles with her clinquant sheen,
And dreamt a life she's ne'er seen.
Dreams breathe wild sans walls around,
From castles in clouds to a realm 'neath crust.
Of tinselled wings to fly off grounds,
To fastest feet to defeat the gust,
And move yet faster than the stormy dust.
Two bread a day with sausages few,
And oft in hunger sleep didn't kiss.
Dreams were weaved oft 'neath the blue,
And quested in 'em she waves of bliss,
Cuz those were moments she could ne'er miss.
A father she had though bacchanal rife,
Lashing women the way he sought.
Her nights stood macabre and so was life,
And heaved she nights in anguish'd thoughts,
Entrapp'd inside a foaming pot.
Bright was the morning; scarlet skies,
Dora walked yards to the solitary dale.
The shimmering river to her aweary eyes,
Spell'd good magic like a faery tale,

And she sang aubades to the passing gale.
Transfixed damsel; Dora the girl,
Glinted bright in broad day light.
She gleamed ablaze as a divine pearl,
And waltzed few blinks in rapt delight,
Oblivious a moment of her hapless plight.
Footfalls loud and louder she heard,
And senses kiss'd her back to dust.
A man; she saw like a predaceous bird,
Scurrying to her and shaking the crust,
His eyes though held no tint of lust.

JOHN TYLER:

Hola damsel! How art thy earthen fate?
Thou veil beaut 'neath sycamores,
Poor thy roots bequeath'd ciphers in crates,
And abysmal noughts adorn thy doors,
Forsaking thy beaut in ghastly shores.
Dora heard words and an eldritch voice,
Wherefore a stranger talks to me? Thought she,
She gazed for moments and heard no noise,
Bewitched she stood beneath a maple tree,
And lost for blinks in a reverie.

JOHN TYLER:

What see'st thou? My countenance?
I'm a man not known to thee.

I'm from the lands where faeries dance,
And wealth is found in brooks for free,
My land's beyond the greatest sea.

JOHN TYLER:

Thou art Dora; thy name sounds sweet,
Thy visage is alluring to good old eyes.
Lips ain't bright and curves ain't neat,
But still thou ows't the brightest skies,
And mime a nymph in mortal disguise.

JOHN TYLER:

I shalt make thou dazzle the world,
And rein as a queen my treasur'd realm.
Yon my lands for years hath call'd,
Thy regal name to savour thy helm,
And I shalt aid thou triumph and whelm.
Dora's eyes with a brighter glance,
Gazed at him as a herald to spring.
She veil'd a grin on her countenance,
And heard the jocund birds to sing,
As they witnessed the benignant king.
Pink and red she blushed all thru',
Her bosoms awoke from aeonian slumber,
Her lips grew bright and grinn'd anew,
And age seemed none but a charming number,
And feet grew strong as an Elmwood lumber.

DORA:

How hast thou but learned my name?
Dora's voice had a dulcet flow.

JOHN TYLER:

I am the Duke and 'tis an elementary game,
And thou hold fruits that deserve to grow,
And triumph each land with an ardent glow.

JOHN TYLER:

I seek no wealth to serve thou bliss,
Just thy pair of bosoms to play.
And the warmth of thy rheumy kiss,
To paint the glimpses of my day,
Won't thou please me the way I say?
The evening looked too cold and bleak,
Flickering stood the candle flame.
Dora was there at the cottage; meek
And heard a voice to call her name,
Come inside! Let's play the game.
Her trembling legs were dubious though,
The cottage was pale and bleakly grime.
The woods look'd macabre as a horror show,
And made her quiver as a direful dream,
Well beneath the faint moonbeams.

The man walked closer and pulled her in,
And kiss'd her lips all at once.
As a hungry hound he lick'd her skin,
And made her surrender to his stance,
And devoured her steamy countenance.
Her curves stood bare; with no attire,
His lustful fingers caressed 'em whole.
And down below the damsel's fire,
Burned his stem and seared his bowl,
As he yearned to trespass her hole.
Hours of moaning ceased too soon,
The man was jocund with gleeful eyes.

JOHN TYLER:

Hey lassie! Behold the yonder moon,
And risqué bosoms of the lustful skies,
We shalt rein 'em but in disguise.

JOHN TYLER:

John: The Duke promises to thee,
A world of wealth and joy profound.
Where goodness reins and mirth wafts free,
And zephyrs blow with a mellifluous sound,
And kiss amour to the souls on ground.

JOHN TYLER:

Dost thou feel'st a need to purge,
The world of sinful ogres around?
Dost thou behold'st the fiendish surge,
Of myriad silhouettes of a hungry hound;
And the roots of humanity sold for pounds?

DORA:

I consent thou! O rever'd duke,
I've seen much brute distress.
Daimons of poverty did rebuke,
Each day with a mangled dress,
And a life of an Augean mess.

JOHN TYLER:

Worry not Dora! Worry not thou,
This regal knight shalt paint thy skies,
And adorn the moments thou art now,
For hours ahead each new surprise,
Shalt wait for thee in sweet disguise.

8. THE INTROSPECTION

Alex and Tyler walks down beach,
And Dora awaits 'em gayly return.
Life is bliss with no bad breach,
But there's so much in life to learn,
And love still is a glory to earn.
Right aft the night in Burming Town,
Tyler left his vengeful oath.
Ne'er e'er his heart doth frown,
Ne'er a word in ire he quoth,
Life gave a meaning and a happy growth.
On Dora's plea he returned last once,
And fetched good money from Gyron's den.
Buried for years seeking a chance,
Were now all good to cater to men,
And serve mankind with noble brains.
Hither on a plot amid the crowded shore,
Tyler launched a stall of choice.
Selling burritos, cakes and more,
He savoured the crowd and gleeful noise,
And savoured much more Dora's voice.
Dora conceived with Tyler's seed,

And soon was set to reap her fruit.
Tyler's child is the hour's need,
To prove to the world a noble root,
With Tyler's mind and Dora's beaut.
Alex stay'd as a friend and guide,
And married he; ne'er as a sacrifice.
He too was happy deeper inside,
And pray'd good Lord of the yonder skies,
With hope and delight in his soulful eyes.
Dora and Tyler worked too hard,
And soared yet higher with passing days.
They learned new life and novice words,
And triumph'd each day with roaring ways,
And earn'd good wealth amid this race.
As a year upon the wheels of time,
Rolled off faster than ever ere,
John now miles away off crime,
Weaved a paradise with his share,
And breathed each day the pristine air.
He ow'th a vehicle with golden rims,
And fancy doors to make it gleam.
He drove off miles with boundless whims,
'Tis all to him appear'd a happy dream,
A sweet reverie beneath moonbeams.
Soon by the grace of Lord divine,
A little boy was born to 'em.
His eyes were bright with a torrid shine,
Adorning well the facial frame.
A handsome boy to a pretty dame.

They christened him as rever'd Zeus,
And taught him lessons from hermit's pages.
He play'd all day thru' grassland dews,
And learn'd his skills from Christian sages,
That Tyler sought since childhood ages.
One fine night when drowsy John,
Embraced Dora with tender arms,
Dora kiss'd him like a fawn,
And lured him wild with her lustful charms,
And pulled him nigh to her bosoms warm.
Then quoth she few words; soft and firm,
Deep into John Tyler's mind.

DORA:

I seek not thy phallus or thy tepid sperm,
But a deed for whole mankind,
A deed that's wise, rever'd and kind.

DORA:

Hear'st me o beloved mate,
Thou art life that Dora respires.
Even though 'tis generous fate,
We must ne'er be slaves to desire,
And burn our souls in infernal fire.

DORA:

We must be too clean and pure,
And a golden soul to eyes of fate.
May we nymphs from heavens; allure,
And make 'em all our beloved mates,
To pour lone happiness in our crates.

DORA:

I beseech to thee one last time,
Carry thyself to the cop's abode.
Squeal to 'em thy days of crime,
And reconcile to the holy Lord,
And seek His mercy with accord.

DORA:

They might take thee captive inside,
And hurl thy bod into the den.
And hither I shalt but hire a guide,
A lawyer best in the world of men,
With agile blood inside his veins.

DORA:

Alex shalt thus aid me long,
And aid thee too with all his might.
And then in days our forces strong,
Shalt grant thee freedom from this plight,
And thus our life shalt dazzle bright.

DORA:

The fates shalt rejoice thy veracity,
And hail thy name with godly delight.
Ne'er e'er their covert enmity,
Send to us those bleak cold nights,
Or anguish'd hours of bereft plights.
Tyler pondered o'er the night,
And quoth no word until the dawn.
He rose with a smile and look'd too bright,
And kiss'd his beloved naughty fawn,
And went for a walk all alone.
Aft an hour he pranced back gay,
And call'd 'em both to hear him say.

JOHN TYLER:

Dear mates; to time thou pray,
And wait for me until a day,
I return proud to this resplendent bay.

JOHN TYLER:

I need no lawyer or thy aids,
Let me face it all alone.
I've savoured all His abundant shades,
Let me now for moments mourn,
And surrender myself to His throne.

JOHN TYLER:

If His arms all mercy drops,
Bestow upon my sinful soul.
I shalt reap more wealthy crops,
And triumph again each mundane goal,
And return hither with His nostrum bowl.

JOHN TYLER:

Let my store to thee; more wealth
Proffer each day; when I'm gone.
Pay good heed to thy humane health,
And worry not o my beloved fawn,
I shalt not be thither alone.

JOHN TYLER:

God shalt aid me in His way,
And I do trust him with all my heart.
Wait hither for that glorious day,
Till then o darling let me depart,
And make my son stout and smart.
Tyler arose and walked in hush,
His tacit footsteps vanished in a blink.
Alex still with his morn's tooth brush,
Got no moment to calmly think,
And ponder more o'er a little drink.

Dora wept for few lone hours,
And felt an ache in her fragile heart.
She moaned aloud 'neath bathroom showers,
Yet failed to accept her husband's depart.
She felt brute stings of a thousand darts.
Alex helplessly consoled though,
He knew there won't be another chance.
The cops are brutes and Tyler's foe,
They might break his countenance,
And kill him with no further glance.

9. THE LAST MISSION

Burming Town

Scene 1

The crowd is thick and a chesty one,
Each one brute and yokelish soul.
No pity they feel as a summer's sun,
Yet adrift prance sans sweeter goals,
Rolling on crust like spherical bowls.
Tyler was clad in mangled attire,
Torn; half woven and stitched too odd.
His shoes were draggled in malodorous mire,
Yet chanting aloud the poems of God,
And swaying to and fro his rusted sword.
Dora still dazzled in a lacerate gown,
Golden strings hung from the tapestry.
She walked forth lone thru' the huddled town,
As a stray protagonist in a garbled story,
Scurrying quests for a paltry glory.
A store by a nook caught glances soon,
Tyler gestured an assentient arm.
They saw the skies with a bleary moon,

Hovering herald of the evening's charm,
The store was right by a barren farm.
Two words he spoke to Dora's ears,
"OUR CLAN" quoth he with fair respite.
The little hotel with too many smears,
Mimed a child with a hapless plight,
Mourning and starving for myriad nights.

JOHN TYLER:

He's Alex! Alex Sky is a brotherly form,
We're mates since ages; decades three.
His agile mind can sniff old storms,
And count the clouds that hover free,
And count the leaves on the redwood tree.

JOHN TYLER:

Alex! She's Dora; a damsel I've search'd all life,
She's brave and smart and enticing a girl.
She's kind and noble and true; a wife,
Her heart's pristine as an ivory pearl.
She's firm to tempests and poised to swirls.

JOHN TYLER:

I trust; thou hast of course this day,
Read and felt each word I wrote.
They're not mere words; allow me say,

I mean each ink as a great man's quote.
Aid me drive this one last boat.

JOHN TYLER:

Know'st thou since ages ere,
Tyler fears no sinful brute.
Nor those wildcats he shalt spare,
Or set 'em free as forbidden fruits,
He must burn their deepest roots.

ALEX SKY:

Good words sate good minds oh dear,
And thus for goodness I honour thee.
O Tyler! What isles hast thou been on ere?
And what's all about thy mate; young Jerry?
Thou hast once unveil'd to me.

JOHN TYLER:

Let not the moon; sink deep and blush,
And hide all night in clouds so dark.
These tales shalt be revealed in hush,
Aft I find the scoundrel's mark,
That one black star amid these sparks.

JOHN TYLER:

This night shalt be but dreams for Brown,
And one last dream; ere he fully sleeps.
We certainly must hunt him down,
And let his beau but perch and weep,
And bury his corpse 'neath the dust; too deep.

JOHN TYLER:

Humans claim the finest art,
And thus too saintly they must be.
Yet few brutes ain't that wise and smart,
And plunge themselves into the sea,
Of fires and thorns and mourning glee.

JOHN TYLER:

Behold o mate! Hither's a blueprint,
Brown's beau is Elisa Woods.
She's too canny and a winner of sprints,
And fetes her alluring womanhood.
To strangers she's oft too rude.

ALEX SKY:

Be cautious while thou chaffer along,
She's smart and sniffs adroit foes.
And entraps 'em all with her amorous songs,
And carry 'em along wheree'r she goes.
Her secret den none still knows.

ALEX SKY:

There's frail a heart and a frailer dot,
The dulcinea is frail to men;
With stout a stature and warmth in thoughts,
And for long can hold his rains,
Riding longer with brute a cane.

JOHN TYLER:

Hold on Alex! Paused great John,
Mean'st thou a whore awaits!
She's a trull and oft alone,
Stung by bleak and brute her fates,
Where no man hath been her mate.

ALEX SKY:

Thou dost hold a mind agile,
Whence these crates of wisdom bide.
Certainly thru' a triumphant mile,
Return'st thou to this countryside,
And be forever my supreme guide.

JOHN TYLER:

Morrow; the thirteenth; and we shalt leave,
Tacitly unto the raven's den.

And thou shalt make the scoundrel heave,
With luscious arts and a little pen,
And forsake the corpse for his doleful men.

DORA:

Impart me the art as I'm but an ignorant soul,
Ne'er a man I'd slain in my hapless life.
A man in skin and flesh and bones; though foul,
Deserves few stabs from a rusted knife,
But fear I still his crafty wife.

JOHN TYLER:

Hither behold! This little tip...
Surrender thy bosoms to his lousy arms.
Let him play; hurl no whip,
Make him frailer in thy charms,
And pierce the quill; quick and warm.

JOHN TYLER:

Kiss his lips until he's cold,
And fall deadpan o'er the floor.
Let his body freeze as gold,
Ere the people crowd the shore,
With their bustling shops and stores.

JOHN TYLER:

Remember! This brute hath ravished timid girls,
Plunder'd poorest men in towns.
Swindled men for phoney pearls,
And nobbled e'en the regal crown,
Clad in attires like a clown.

JOHN TYLER:

His evil beloved rook'd young men,
For lustful moments quite a few.
Alluring 'em to her secret den,
Entrapp'd 'em whole with tricks anew,
And thus her penny in banks too grew.

JOHN TYLER:

I shalt be but a client to her,
Seeking favours to quench my thirst.
And a single night for a million dollars,
Ne'er sounds too bleak and worst,
She must dance amuck on dust.

JOHN TYLER:

And I shalt too do my secret art,
And make her moan too loud and wild.
And pierce the woman's sweetest part,

And let her bleed until she's mild,
And her lips in my elixir beguiled.
The sun look'd bold and so were they,
The morning grinn'd a knavish smile.
Alex wished 'em a fortune's day,
And walked with 'em a little mile.
And wished 'em triumph with a solemn wile.

Scene 2

JOHN TYLER:

(DISGUISED AS AN IMAGINARY CHARACTER "BRAWN GYLER")

Blissful morning I wish to thee,
O gentle soul; I'm hither to serve.
This is Brawn Gyler; thou mustn't know me,
As I sell these regional garbs,
And seek great people to scribble blurbs.

JOHN TYLER:

What is thy name o madame grace?
How may I address thee?

Thou ow'st the prettiest human face,
And a woman lush in smoking spree,
Spreading around a dust of glee.

ELISA WOODS:

Hola young man! Mr mmmm; Gyler right?
What garb hast thou brought for me?
How but at this morning bright;
Find'st thou my secret sea?
Who's unveil'd my den to thee?

JOHN TYLER:

Harry! Knowest thou his name guess I,
Of all the agile minds of north.
He's a buddy and his door's too nigh,
And I dwell by the Henry's Garth,
A town of happy souls in mirth.

ELISA WOODS:

Ow! Harry is a mate to me and more,
He's reveal'd all tales I trust.
There're splendid nights that we explore,
And he keeps riding all for lust,
And I lay tacit to his thrust.

ELISA WOODS:

He makes me moan the loudest still,
My husband ne'er ever so rode.
His member's smart as an ebony hill,
And many a crop in me he sowed,
His soul still bides in my abode.

ELISA WOODS:

Dost thou ride? O Gyler dear?
Art thou a man of power and strength?
Hast thou sated a woman's layer?
And triumph'd the game with thy length?
Or just bare words bear thy strength?

JOHN TYLER:

Hither I am o voluptuous girl,
I'll make thee a damsel riding hard.
Shed thy doubts and feel my swirl,
Thy moans thru' these walls shalt be well heard,
And I shalt fathom thy abyssal lard.

JOHN TYLER:

Thy bosoms shalt dance and so shalt we,
To each tide that soars within our caves.
And as li'l coasters amid the sea,

We shalt fete as amorous slaves,
Captive to lust and lustful graves.
Tyler groped the damsel close,
Somewhere in late twenties she,
Curves quite cusped as she arose,
And hairs too blonde as a seething sea,
Her skin turn'd red in lustful glee.
The gown she wore was stripped too soon,
All in lingerie she stood too still.
The buxom blonde gleamed as the moon,
And her chest seemed stout as an acuate hill,
And she's all keen for the strenuous drill.
The room had curtains; cool and bright,
Dense tapestries were hung all o'er.
The walls had paints; too smooth and light,
And all adorned was the central door,
And dazzling tiles had draped the floor.
Tyler's eyes for a blink or two,
Scanned all thru' the damsel's den.
Her eyes had lashes and they're true,
He wonder'd the count of shameless men,
Who lay entrapp'd amid this ben.
Aft an hour or perhaps few more,
As those scoundrels lay deadpan,
Elisa like an evil whore,
Invites in her brutal clan.
They lash dark blue the aweary man.
They plunder all his wealth and skin,
And plunge him off on barren roads.

And as he runs from the moment's sin,
Two silhouettes follow the ways he strode,
Until they find his true abode.
For months a few the duncish man,
Faces threats thru' letters grim.
And by the time he's chummy clan,
Gets to hear his blaring scream,
His tale fades off as a bygone dream.
Such were preys with a soaring number,
And naive those men were slayed each hour.
She played well pitches to steal their slumber,
And plunged 'em off as wilted flowers,
Miles away from their gemutlich bowers.
Soon the damsel warm on bed,
Rode well agog o'er Tyler's tower.
And deeper he went as lone he fed,
Deluge of elixirs e'ery hour,
Into the damsel's vacuous bower.
For quarter the morn amid those walls,
Sly the damsel moaned each blink.
She savoured well each Tyler's swirl,
Way more delighted than she could think.
She quaff'd his seed as a bracing drink.
And when the weary sun yawned wide,
Amid the roseate arms of dusk,
A little needle was pierced inside,
Masquerading a phallus draped in mask.
Thus was planned the brutal task.
Her moans; turn'd groans and one last cry,

And then she wilted still on crust.
Her eyes yearned words ere death came nigh,
'Twas vengeance and a broken trust.
Lady Woods must returneth to dust.
And all bonds broken; all debts pay'd,
A moment of life and still mankind,
Brags of wealth and castles made,
But ne'er a spiritual piece of mind.
All men are eejit and all men are blind.
Tyler for a moment thought in hush,
And thus was lost in senses beyond.
Where's true heaven and where's bleak cuss?
And who weaves feelings and threads these bonds?
And then he saw the defunct bod of the damsel blonde.
He scurried a blink and ere more men,
Reached the ebony roads to trade,
He waited by the great fountain,
Amid the woods where the flocks still play'd,
And little the darkness of the evening sway'd.
Tyler's mind still foamed and surged,
In melancholy it gasped few times.
Is it true that guilt hath purged;
The blemishes that hath play'd brute chimes?
And forced his arms to dreadful crimes?
He mourned faintly with soft moans few,
And all that danced were memories grave.
The old wood house where Tyler grew,
Kept him always like a slave,
Shackled within an ebony cave.

SCENE 3

(REMINISCENCE)

Long eons back when the moon was white,
And sky was lilac; smiling rife.
Tyler too had tender nights,
And gayly breathed his mortal life,
And play'd thru' fields his soothing fife.
A mother he had with a kind visage,
Who'd served him food and care.
And served him love till a certain age,
He'd learned to grab his share,
And felt the voice of the air.
Great lessons earned he till a ten,
Ten long years beneath safe shades.
A brutal father each day to the den,
Carried along no tinge of bread,
But a world of evils and dread.
His drunken eyes would ravish each girl,
And arms were raised to lash the child.
And whip more brute like a tempest swirl,
The only wife who's calm and mild,
And e'en aft trouncing; neatly smiled.
Aft a decade when Tyler's ten,

JOHN TYLER

His poor mother left all that's earth.
Higher into the celestial den,
Perhaps as a maiden in heaven's garth,
She savoured the days in divine mirth.
Hither down in this anguish'd cave,
Tyler quaff'd more torment rife.
Whips and lashes like a slave,
Coerc'd him blame his dire life,
Too aweary a little boy in strife.
His knavish daddy a damsel brought,
Blooming pink in youthful attire.
He spared no hour to a second thought,
And plunged little Tyler into the mire.
The woman dazzled in lustful fire.
He witnessed moments prurient though,
Ne'er meant for a little boy.
His naive mind still learned to grow,
All alone like a broken toy.
A bleak childhood sans puerile joy.
Oft a while they fed no food,
The little child kept starving days.
They feted hours in lustful moods,
And made good love in a hundred ways.
The wean kept rambling thru' the place.
Four lone years hath play'd in haste,
Tyler witnessed worst each day.
He could see but a broken nest,
Crumbling down like a fragile clay,
Losing on each a bit of hay.

He saw mountains frowning rife,
And clouds were all too bleak and grey.
And hither his dad's novice wife,
Flail'd him brute e'ery day,
And he'd ne'er a word to say.
One fine night he heard fresh moans,
As his father made overt love.
The floor kept shaking and Tyler alone,
Beheld in hush the skies above,
And felt himself as a wingless dove.
His anguish and thus grave disdain,
Transformed as an ireful storm.
Little John now all insane,
Scurried tacitly into the dorm,
And just in a blink broke each saintly norm.
A dagger he had still fresh and red,
Gory two bods lay defunct and still.
The earthen floor was all so flooded,
The corpses lay as crumbled hills,
Void of life and humane skills.
Not a moment waited; he,
And scampered in haste to the yonder leas,
Miles beyond the cops could see,
He blended with the southern breeze,
And hid himself; amid the trees.
The night came dreary; dark and cold,
The winter woods were freezing white.
The mountains stood like a hermit old,
With ivory beards and a wise insight,

Vowing each moment to the regal night.
Tyler quiver'd until a cave found; he,
And nestled for a moment sans a voice.
The darkness thither like an ebony sea,
Foamed and surged without a noise,
And Tyler perched with a saintly poise.
Wild wolves howled and snakes hiss'd loud,
Croaking frogs too rambled fast.
The skies were dark with seething clouds,
And Tyler heaved in cold aghast,
Perching o'er the frozen crust.
The night was long but wilted too,
And morning sun was all anew.
The life he had; too bleak and blue,
Now stands yonder as a bygone beau,
As petals of memories with a fading hue.
He beheld in awe the peaks of gold,
As the snow gleamed 'neath sunbeams.
The zephyr too came soft and cold,
And drenched him whole like nebule streams.
'Twas all alike as fantasy dreams.
He walked thru' stones to climb the tor,
And climb'd each slope with ebony rocks.
A new life; though like a pleasant war,
Thru' hills and woods and unbounded flocks,
Hearing around tempestuous knocks.
Soon by mid-day as the sun went high,
And soothing gales were ruffling thru',
Tyler saw the towns were nigh,

And the yonder sky seemed brighter blue,
This world for him was all anew.
As by the roads of the novice town,
He walked timidly figuring scenes,
Hunger stung him up and down;
And groaned he bleak sans ample means,
And found two cents in his lacerate jeans.
Thither a shop was selling aloud,
Chicken burritos hot on flames,
Six dollars quoth he; bright and loud,
Tyler but play'd hunger games,
Ne'er heareth he these wealthy names.

JOHN TYLER:

Hola Sir, lend'st me thy ears a while,
Hear'st me; I implore to thee.
Let me with thy kindest smile,
Have a little bite for free,
For days I'm but a starving tree.

JOHN TYLER:

I've hither two cents two offer,
Just two cents and nothing more.
I may serve thee as a chauffeur,
And open for thee thy vehicle's door,
And sell for thee by the northern shore.
The tradesman look'd for seconds few,

Gazed too close at Tyler's face.

UNCLE GYRON (GYRON FELLIX):

Thou look eldritch; a visage so new,
O boy unveil thy roots and race.
Prove thou ain't a grim disgrace.

JOHN TYLER:

I beseech to thee o generous soul,
I'm just a child searching life.
A nomad in town sans certain goals,
Just two cents and a little fife,
This tale unveils my mortal strife.

JOHN TYLER:

I know not roots nor race to speak,
Brute a daddy for a life I had.
A sweet mother though frail and weak,
Mourned each blink; too bleak and sad,
Quite tormented by my dad.

JOHN TYLER:

One fine day the poor woman,
Left us all to the world of stars.
She left behind no gemulitch clan,

But a daddy with countless scrapes and scars,
And to starve few empty jars.

JOHN TYLER:

My father espoused another girl,
And brought her home too soon.
I being a wean couldn't bear the swirl,
And was thrashed to the yonder moon.
And heaved I oft amid those facinorous goons.

UNCLE GYRON:

Stop now o dear little boy; stop, stop, stop!
I can't hear thy anguish'd past; no anymore,
Such an innocent soul thou art; a verdant crop,
And thy daddy such a brute and the lady a whore,
Come in o sweetest soul; this is thy door.

UNCLE GYRON:

Not one but as much as thou seek,
Burritos! They're all for thee.
Laugh now! Be not coy and meek,
Thou ain't shackled but as birds; free,
Behold! The world's but an abysmal sea.

UNCLE GYRON:

Behind the store my home awaits,
Little two rooms and an aisle to rest.
I stay all alone with fates,
And breed good moments in my nest,
No stern command; no brute behest.

UNCLE GYRON:

Thou art quite as a son to me;
A little wean that must now laugh.
Best a life now waits for thee,
All good potables must thou quaff,
Miles away from hills and tuff.

UNCLE GYRON:

Uncle Gyron thou may address,
Gyron Felix they nam'd me gay.
And little by this shrubs of cress,
I do spend my quarter day,
Oft too idle; no man to play.

UNCLE GYRON:

I sell burritos and few more,
Sales still sink and way to drown.
No man so stops by my door,
As they drive past to yonder towns,
And I still wait till the sun goes down.

JOHN TYLER:

Uncle Gyron! Feed'st me a bite,
And I shalt paint thy shop in glee.
Dull thy doors must gleam too bright,
And allure men too nigh for free,
All for kindness and no fee.
Tyler gulped few bites and more,
Until he felt too sated again.
Quite too soon those bleak old doors,
Look'd bewitching to the passing men.
The sluggish store now smiled again.
Gyron gazed with gobsmacked eyes,
O what beat thou carry o boy?
Thou art a star amid yonder skies,
Thou ain't meek, frail or coy,
But a crate of mirth and endless joy.
For years a few by the garth of cress,
Tyler stay'd as a sweet young man.
Sharing work and healing stress,
He aided old Gyron in his plans,
As the only heir from his aeonian clans.
One night when the skies were white,
And snowfall draped each road all wide.
Winters hovered o'er the bleak cold night,
And frozen zephyrs kiss'd e'ery side,
Gyron quiver'd and feebly cried.

UNCLE GYRON:

O boy! Hither com'st thou; hear'st me one last,
Riding o'er wheels of time, I've reach'd the shore,
All debts pay'd off; no debt from the past,
Still knocks on my earthen door.
I've counted hours and they ain't a lot more.

UNCLE GYRON:

All wealth earned and all wealth stored,
Art safely concealed behind the frames.
Till this day each worth thy scored;
Is nuff for me to hail thy name,
Thou art triumphant! Tis thy game.
Tyler gazed sans words much loud,
His voice was frail in mournful winds.
Bleak seem'd skies and each dark cloud,
Ruffled past the remaining ruins,
Punishing Tyler like brutal queens.
The corpse lay still ahead of him,
Uncle Gyron left for a life.
'Twas all like a dreadful dream,
Of wounds and flesh and blood stain'd knife,
The world ahead now whispers strife.

DORA:

Dora's voice was shriller more,

O duke! Where hast thou been lost all while?
The wonderland or Gryffindor?
Behold! Tis dusk and the remaining miles
Must be trod with skill and guile.

DORA:

I've done my work too well and good,
The evil soul is way too far.
Let me brag my womanhood,
I'm too bright as the northern star,
Or with brave men I'm at par.
Tyler quoth no words yet then,
In hush of the evening walk'd he lone.
His eyes had tears and a covert pain,
And Tyler now seem'd all unknown.
Dora heard him muttering alone.
Few lone miles thru' the autumn's woods,
Both 'em walk'd yet spoke no word.
But by the edge where the slums all stood,
Dora squeak'd as a wounded bird,
And Tyler now her noises heard.
Tyler smiled like a child all gay,
And pull'd her closer all at once.
He kiss'd her lips like an amorous play,
And gave himself another chance,
To play and love and sing and dance.
He grabb'd her bosoms firm again,
And kiss'd 'em both with all delight.

For good blinks he lost his pain,
And celebrated the lustful night.
Dora look'd racy, warm and bright.
Soon on the crust where leaves all lay,
Dora and Tyler made good love.
His phallus grew strong to creep and prey,
And clouds were all too dark above,
Awaiting to shower the rain of love.
Aft an hour when all job's good,
And sated well were both love birds,
They rose again in a gleeful mood,
And pranced back quiet sans voice or words,
Savouring the moment as rattling nerds.
Soon they stood by Alex's door,
Triumphant both still quoth no word.
Tyler look'd too frail and sore,
Too wilted a man as a wingless bird,
Trembling oft too thru' the yard.
Alex with a wide smile greeted 'em both,
And call'd 'em in to perch and rest.
Yet John Tyler; no words he quoth,
And look'd too weary sans good zest,
As a horse too sick off stern behest.

ALEX SKY:

O dear compadre! What troubles thee more?
I see darkness draping thy face.
Ain't thou triumphant? Wherefore sore?

Art thou weary of a tiresome race?
Or careworn off thy criminal chase?
Tyler gazed for little a while,
And spoke few words though low and frail.

JOHN TYLER:

I'm aweary of this same old mile,
This seems to me as an ebony cell,
Cuss'd I am in my own sweet dale.

JOHN TYLER:

I felt blest when brutes I slay'd,
And drenched myself in redness wild.
Many a deal I crack'd and play'd,
Oft too cruel and seldom mild,
What variance exists if sin still smiled?

JOHN TYLER:

Thou know'st truth and all my past,
And all that's true from earth to the moon.
All bygone can't turn to dust,
And sleep forever like a sunken dune,
Or disappear like a bypast tune.

JOHN TYLER:

Winds of past still ruffle and waft,
And bring forth scents from defunct yore.
Uncle Gyron's sombre craft,
Still as a memory haunts my door,
And gnaws me sharp within my core.

JOHN TYLER:

All these years for truth I bled,
And slay'd good men for nobler causes.
And for sinners a world of dread,
I'd made of deadly hemlock doses,
And trod I still; on briary roses.

JOHN TYLER:

This day but had a tale of difference,
And a gust of ardent emotion came.
It turn'd me down as a saintly reference,
And gave me a novice golden frame,
To adorn my picture and fete good fame.

JOHN TYLER:

Moments ere when drilled I deep,
And screw'd the lewd a couple of times.
I ne'er felt I'll put her sleep,
And fete another triumphant crime,
And dance amuck to glorious chimes.

JOHN TYLER:

Years before by the dales of west,
I met a man of skills and flairs.
His arms would work and work for best,
And work unknown to evil affairs,
And work like an adept for wholesome shares.

JOHN TYLER:

I made him slave to the buried desires,
And used his art to purge ill ones.
I helped 'em all to reach the mires,
And ascertained no more fairest chance,
But to stale and decay and heave in trance.
Alex beheld the frowning face,
When Tyler quoth his dreadful past,
He burned each blink in true disgrace,
And heaved in remorse and distorted trust.
Tyler fell o'er the earthen dust.

JOHN TYLER:

"Mercy! O for mercy hither I beseech,
Hear'st thou o Lord of death."
Tyler cried and embraced a twitch,
And soon was void of healthy breath,
Yet kept imploring with his faith.

Dora pulled his quivering bod,
And wrapp'd him warm in her tepid arms.
She pray'd too ardent to the Lord,
And kiss'd him with her graceful charms,
Soon his skin was still and warm.
For hours he slept and knew no tale,
Dora kept serving all her love.
Alex too still shook his scale,
And gazed deadpan at those clouds above,
Dora look'd sombre like a dove.
Aft few hours she walk'd straight though,
And sought few answers from Mr Sky,

DORA:

Who's he real? Where did he grow?
Isn't he a Duke? Was that a lie?
Why did he lie? Tell me why?

ALEX SKY:

Hey damsel! I'm gonna tell thee all that's true,
And all that's fair and for great good.
He's not a duke but a Prince of the blue,
And that he had a bleak childhood,
Small in a cottage beyond the woods.

ALEX SKY:

His dearly mother though left too soon,
His loathsome daddy thrashed him whole.
He brought home a damsel like a boon,
Yet baneful and with wicked goals,
She loved him ne'er and wracked his soul.

ALEX SKY:

He slay'd 'em both and one good night,
Scarpered bibulous into the woods.
And scurried beyond the people's sight,
Carrying along his lorn childhood.
He lived for days sans penny or food.

ALEX SKY:

Fortune favoured at last and smiled,
And reached he; adrift to a burritos store.
Uncle Gyron; coy and mild,
Loved him aft he heard him more,
And for Tyler opened his door.

ALEX SKY:

Life took turns and luck kiss'd grace,
As fortune fed him until few years.
Triumphant felt he in this race,
And forgot his past that stood with tears,
Like a car with broken gears.

ALEX SKY:

One fine day when he was twenty four,
And life was savouring; cool and bright,
Gyron left this earthen floor,
And disappeared amid the night,
Much beyond this humane sight.

ALEX SKY:

Tyler mourned for two full days,
And wept he; hard as a little child.
He had wealth much that pays,
For lavish a life; yet he ne'er smiled,
Nor celebrated his days too wild.

ALEX SKY:

He fetched all wealth and dug deep holes,
And buried in 'em the greater share.
And took off some for unknown goals,
And vanished into the thinnest air,
And ne'er turned back to fetch more share.

ALEX SKY:

As nomads he moved thru' barren lands,
Thru' meadows wide and long bare dales.

And searched good work thru' brooks and sands,
As he pranced thru' wilder gales,
And sojourned for whiles on chartreuse vales.

ALEX SKY:

One and a half decades ere though,
I was a chauffeur to the elite men.
I drove 'em all like a parade show,
And lived all lone in a befouled den,
Somewhere amid the Houston's Fen.

ALEX SKY:

A bright day though with smiling skies,
And I drove past the scarlet woods.
The road was bare; with butterflies,
And one did perch o'er my vehicle's hood,
It look'd so elegant; saintly good.

ALEX SKY:

The mustang ran sans riders one,
And I alone drove past the town.
I saw yon skies and found a sun,
Smiling gaily and gazing down,
To trace the only driving clown.

ALEX SKY:

Destined to the yonder bay,
A relative was about to come.
I drove yet faster thru' the day,
With the music of the drum.
I drove past woods and cottages some.

ALEX SKY:

Soon thither o'er the barren roads,
Saw I; a mighty timber log.
And like a gust few gleaming swords,
Stopped my way all like a fog.
They barked aloud as hungry dogs.

ALEX SKY:

They yelled raucously; clamorous too,
Abandon thou this vehicle now.
Speak not a word; not one nor few,
Take to the woods like a clever cow,
Turn not behind! Leav'st thou.

ALEX SKY:

I scurried behind to save my soul,
And dashed suddenly with a man.
A young man stood like an iron ball,

As if a part of a warrior clan.
His chin was stout and hairs were tan.

ALEX SKY:

He gestured me to the thickets hide,
And pranced too bold to the men in black.
He lashed 'em all as a jocund ride,
And filled 'em all in nylon sacks.
They groaned aloud with a hundred cracks.

ALEX SKY:

A hero he is! I muttered in awe,
And beheld him proudly return to me.
He smiled with wounds too fresh and raw,
And paused beneath a rosewood tree,
And spoke few words in rever'd glee.

ALEX SKY: (QUOTING JOHN TYLER'S WORDS WHILE NARRATING THE HAPPENINGS FROM THE SHORE OF THE PAST.)

Rise; oh mate! Thy road's too clean,
And vehicle still is safe and bright.
Drive again; the woods art green,
Pass the woods ere comes the night,
And ghosts come live 'neath frail moonlight.

ALEX SKY:

He laugh'd aloud and pulled me high,
And as he began to walk behind.
I called him louder 'neath the sky,
And tried to read his eldritch mind,
Till the depths my soul could find.

ALEX SKY: (WORDS HE SPOKE TO JOHN TYLER WHEN THEY FIRST MET).

Grateful I am profoundly to thee,
But how is it to pass unknown?
While in perils thou savest me,
And walking off all alone?
Let thyself be to me well known.

ALEX SKY: (QUOTING TYLER'S WORDS FROM THE PAGES OF PAST).

He smiled a tinge and quoth too mild,
I'm John Tyler; a man from the west.
These woods seem perilous, dark and wild,
Let's scurry off past in sincere haste,
And chaffer things we love the best.

ALEX SKY:

Come inside and let me serve,

I shalt drive thee off the woods.
I'm still quivering; frail mine nerves,
We must have some drinks and food,
And spend the evening real good.

ALEX SKY: (QUOTING TYLER)

What's thy name o smarter soul?
How but earn thee food and breath?
Is this chariot thy property whole?
Or someone else's noble faith?
Trust me but I'm not a brutal wraith.

ALEX SKY:

I'm Alex; Alex Sky is what they named,
A chauffeur I am; driving roads.
A vehicle of the regal realms; golden framed,
Golden Chasis; resistant to those metal swords,
And locked entirely by secret codes.

ALEX SKY: (QUOTING THE CONVERSATION BETWEEN ALEX AND JOHN THAT HAPPENED IN PAST).

The Duke of Timothy ow'th the wheels,
The hood hath diamond fixed so well.
Cold winds soothe when summer kills,
And tepid air for the winter's bell.

Future weathers it can foretell.

ALEX SKY:

A hundred miles per hour it goes,
But ne'er a jerk thou shalt e'er feel.
Off roads thru' hills; all roads it knows,
And goes on smooth with a profound zeal,
Driving it though ain't big deal.

ALEX SKY:

That was it and then as mates,
We two travelled miles as one.
And all that's past and future fates,
Were unveil'd steady beneath the sun,
And beneath the moon in glee and fun.

ALEX SKY:

For half a decade we stay'd together,
And earned our food the way we could.
I drove wheels and he did leather,
And life was all too smooth and good,
A genuine bond of brotherhood.

ALEX SKY:

Sometimes 'tis not blood that builds,

Bonds that last a life and more.
Two souls may still together yield,
Best of fruits on a barren shore.
Yet ne'er share a common core.

ALEX SKY:

'Tis all on trust and thoughts we share,
And minds that dance to a rhythm pure.
'Tis bond that's green and free as air,
And play a nostrum to heal and cure,
With love and promises sans censure.
Dora smiled and blushed a while,
And maundered soft in a timid voice.

DORA:

I know Mr Sky; I've read his smile,
And thus do swash my endearing choice,
He's music amidst a clamorous noise.

DORA:

A girl certainly reads the story,
A man hides inside his eyes.
The agony covert behind his glory,
Is pellucid as the morning skies,
Though he plays a smart disguise.

DORA:

His sombre smile and subtle tears,
Ne'er can befool a beloved girl-
Whose heart skips beats; in unknown fear-
Of dreadful winds and deadly swirls,
Or alluring traps of wicked churls.

DORA:

She reads her man the way none can,
And loves him true as a devoted soul.
She prays each moment for her man,
For, just a worth that's true and whole,
And a little time that's ne'er foul.

ALEX SKY:

Certainly girl! Tyler of course is nice and true,
And worth thy love and tender care.
He's seen dark tombs and ogres new,
And bled each day to fetch his share,
And triumph'd the battles where triumph was rare.

ALEX SKY:

Trust his eyes; they ne'er would lie,
At least to a girl his heart chased miles.
Thou art abysmal as a whole night sky,

Adorned in stars and a moon with smiles,
An honest smile sans tricks and guiles.

ALEX SKY:

Once upon a time; quoth he,
Poetry served him catholicons.
Wounds o'er ages like a procellous sea,
Made him perch and mourn alone,
Beneath the skies of despondent dawn.

ALEX SKY:

He wrote few lines like verses old,
And ne'er display'd it e'er to men.
He read 'em loud to graves too cold,
And read it to meadows across the fen,
And kept it conceal'd inside his den.
Dora gazed too blank and white,
And asked him questions a few more.

DORA:

He claim'd a duke as an erudite,
And brought me off my native door,
And tested well my girlish core.

DORA:

Is it all for love and care?
Or for lust that a man holds true?
Will he e'er tie knots in prayers?
And make me whole his beloved beau?
Or 'tis all an oneiric view?

ALEX SKY:

Dear girl; thou hear'st me now,
Let me to thee well explain.
Tyler starves for a genuine vow,
A vow of love sans bleak disdain,
He seeks true love as pure as rain.

ALEX SKY:

He hath left his seed in thee,
And thus awaits his fruits too soon.
Little Tyler in a world that's free,
Must come too blest as the graceful moon,
And as a herald to a roaring boon.

ALEX SKY:

He hath served his choices dark,
Years ere in the dales of north.
Many a brute that his mind did mark,
Those too parlous on this earth,
Were hurled miles off this blissful garth.

ALEX SKY:

But as new battles fought on earth,
Calls for a smaller sacrifice.
Few innocent souls those starved in dearth,
Were slay'd off world to the yonder skies,
They knew no sin yet paid a price.

ALEX SKY:

The artist whose great art he used,
Ran miles amuck in grave remorse.
He warned too rife and e'en abused,
But Tyler ran as a thirsty horse,
Beating each one thru' the lone racecourse.

ALEX SKY:

Jerry; the artist lost all good thoughts,
And dug his tomb in endless rue.
He buried himself off battles fought,
And vanished forever into the blue,
Offering the cops some little clue.

ALEX SKY:

They besieged from dales the mighty brook,
And Tyler stood right between the flows.

They had great guns and browned-off looks,
And eyes had ire and an ireful glow,
But Tyler befooled 'em off the show.

ALEX SKY:

He swam off roads thru' the river wide,
And reached a bank; large miles apart.
Aweary Tyler rode on tides,
And kept alive his wizened heart,
And clung too firm to a defunct hart.

ALEX SKY:

He cloaked for days and dwelled in woods,
Still poems he wrote as letters to me.
I swashed for hours his great manhood,
And guts as mighty as the sea,
And as firm as a great old tree.
Dora arose and 'tween she voiced,
And gestured him to pause a while.
Alex gazed bit vexed yet poised,
And forced his lips to calmly smile.
He's harried a little but held no guile.

DORA:

A question seek I; asked she again,
There's a void; a gap or a missing link.

I really wish thou might explain
The roots, there's something we must think,
Something grave behind his blink.

DORA:

May I summarise all sequences fresh?
May I travel back little eons?
I've learn'd of a childhood in disgrace,
I've learn'd of a journey all alone.
I've learn'd of bleak nights and macabre dawns.

DORA:

I've learn'd of Gyron's Burito's store,
I've learn'd of a rising for years a few.
I've learn'd of searching all new shores,
And meeting thee thru' the woods anew,
And a tale of friendship that gayly grew.

DORA:

I've learn'd of days by the northern dale,
Where Tyler; preyed o'er criminals brute.
I've learn'd of an artist whose arms doth hale,
And painted swathes of forbidden fruits,
To allure sinners thru' a delusory chute.

DORA:

But hither awaits a dubious blank,
A doubt that's still swaying in air.
What made Tyler embrace black,
And hunt down criminals bizarre?
'Tis certainly not for a bantam pecuniary share.

DORA:

If not penny then what desire?
What choices made him insane?
Like as cops though sans attire,
He invited a crate of pain,
And chased off sinful men.

DORA:

What purpose I don't well perceive?
What purpose made me firm?
Forsaking a life that I believe,
Could've been too warm,
And blest with a lavish charm.

ALEX SKY:

Alex smiled and quoth then he,
Dora, hear'st thou the truth.
Tyler heaved for years unfree,

And mourned a wasted youth,
His childhood wasn't smooth.

ALEX SKY:

Grudge kept foaming all his life,
For, a man who claimed his father.
He's for him a venomous knife,
Or more of a deadly weather,
He gasped each blink together.

ALEX SKY:

He saw him lash his mother each day,
And hurl all wines at her visage.
He saw in agony but couldn't e'er say,
Few louder words of rage,
But scribbled wild arts on a page.

ALEX SKY:

He'd always burned in flames,
Of vengeance and grave ire.
Little his eyes witnessed mayhems,
And flared with an unseen fire,
But veiled his wild desires.

ALEX SKY:

He counted days to grow up young,
And grab each sinful brute.
And stab 'em all with a dagger strong,
Or serve 'em venomous fruits,
Just to slay 'em off their roots.

ALEX SKY:

As fire to winds; his innocent eyes-
Beheld his mother; quiver wild.
He howled too loud to the boundless skies,
And moaned as a helpless child,
His mother kept quivering wild.

ALEX SKY:

Mid by the night when the moon was nigh,
And the stars were clad in white.
His saw his mother heave and die,
And wilt to the arms of the night.
He wept to this pathetic plight.

ALEX SKY:

Next with the morn when the sun rose high,
And the skies were bright and blue.
Tyler's dad returned; too sly,
With tears more like bleak cold dew,
And a pall that looked too new.

ALEX SKY:

As a haunted dream or a bleak nightmare,
Tyler recalled each ghastly scene.
His brutal dad hath beyond repair,
Slapp'd his mother black and green,
And broke her bones; frail and thin.

ALEX SKY:

Knocked he down her wailing frame,
And fell she; down on crust.
His virile feet sans a tinge of shame,
Crush'd her whole to the dust.
And broke her like frail rust.

ALEX SKY:

Forsaking her die he left off soon,
And ne'er returned thru' the night.
He returned home with the bygone moon,
To savour her anguish'd plight,
And entomb her 'neath bright daylight.

ALEX SKY:

What less must then a criminal do?
Rather he's brute; too grave.

And Tyler; still like a speechless few,
Heaved as a feeble slave,
He's not as strong and brave.

ALEX SKY:

Days two later this savage soul,
Brought home; a witch to fuck.
All day long he knew her hole,
And screw'd her all amuck,
And celebrated his tinselled luck.

ALEX SKY:

Insolent he ne'er bothered to hide-
His fetishes from his heir.
All unveiled his seeds inside,
And moans were all in air,
And a phallus that swayed all bare.

ALEX SKY:

They kept him starving for long hours,
Until he; fell comatose.
Tyler grew like a wilted flower,
Death seem'd well too close,
And poetry mimed dull prose.

ALEX SKY:

How sound a mind despite this all;
Dost thou feel one hold?
His nerves were frail and lost their call,
And his life was bleak and cold.
As if to death 'twas sold.

ALEX SKY:

Either kill or sleep in graves,
Two roads sought him choose.
He chose the one of smarter slaves,
With streaks of crimson hues,
And a solitary life to muse.

ALEX SKY:

Thus to himself a promise he made,
Crime must be inhumed.
And criminals must be purged instead,
And their mires shalt be perfumed,
Or with incense fumed.

ALEX SKY:

Innocent men must live in peace,
And work the way they seek.
They must brood in utmost ease,

And breathe though they're meek,
Or wizened and frail and weak.

ALEX SKY:

Thus an oath did Tyler take,
And surrendered his hours and days.
No purpose or no worthy stake,
Ow'th he from this race,
Just a gleeful heart and a smiling face.
Dora smiled yet a dubious frown,
Muffled the brighter spark.
She muttered a while gazing down,
And then into the dark,
She gazed; as if she searched a mark.

ALEX SKY:

Ye cool girl? What bothers thee?
Ain't thy incertitude effaced forever?
Reveal thy concern; unveil to me,
I carry Tyler's tales as a boundless river,
I can't see thou with dubiety shiver.

DORA:

'Tis no dubiety dear rever'd crony,
Concerned I am with brutal fates.
Purpose might be noble yet sounds irony,

And might send ogres or facinorous mates,
To befool him into the devil's crate.

ALEX SKY:

Worry not sister; I'm still at life,
And till I breathe no fate can harm.
Let him awake and be his wife,
And soothe him always with thy charms,
And protect him with thy divine arms.

10. DORA'S TRIAL

Lambert Island

DORA:

John! Where hast thou plann'd the deal?
No facts yet art unveil'd to me.
What's this place? Warm I feel,
And circumambient is the abysmal sea,
Art we captive or art we free?

JOHN TYLER:

O dulcinea! We art free as birds in the skies,
And brooks down mountain lands,
Each plan shalt be but a game of dice,
And veil'd beneath inscrutable sands,
And some art veil'd 'neath rainbow bands.

JOHN TYLER:

Hither's a riddle for thou to break,
Decrypt the words as smooth they flow.

The page holds age as an oldest cake,
And the ink holds pity but the frail'st glow,
Read at ease; nay fast but slow.

JOHN TYLER:

(RIDDLE)

"Three legs down and three still west,
The blueness hides in green eiderdown.
There're raw beams and a barren chest,
And agile a man from the people's town,
Must find it bright behind the clown."

JOHN TYLER:

Read it twice; thrice or more,
The ink ain't bright yet can be read.
And now thy mind must quest the shore,
And reach the land as has been said,
Scurry o girl ere the ink marks fade.
She read more times and walked alone,
Three legs down! So three legs south,
And three legs right she reach'd a stone,
The great green stone with an open mouth,
Had lain for years o'er the lands of drouth.
The stone face was so a face too strange,
And like a clown on earth it lay-

Just a head and a bare wide grange,
A clown's head no words did say,
And lay so still half sunk in clay.

DORA:

(TALKING TO HERSELF)

"Holy Jesus! What saw mine eyes?"
The poor damsel quiver'd aghast!
A stone or a skull in stony disguise?
Thought she gazing thru' the sterile crust.
There's more inside the hazel dust.
She read again with a loathful frown,
A line still play'd a children's game.
"The blueness hides in green eiderdown",
So might be something 'neath the frame,
The chartreuse duvet's flossy frame.
Wow! A shovel lay right beside,
Tinselled scoop and a handle tall.
Take it Dora! Spoke the guide,
A voice from within her twitchy soul.
She paused a moment like a feeble doll.
Back a length behind the stone,
Delved her shovel deep inside.
She heard herself her feeble moan,
Yet went on drudging far and wide,
And delved the earth from e'ery side.

Half a feet and inches three,
There beneath the hazel earth.
A diamond sparkled all in glee,
And blushed too blue amid the garth.
The diamond lay with a covert worth.
In joy she danced and danced in joy,
And took the diamond safely thence,
And scurried behind to the Tyler boy,
Jumping o'er each wall and fence.
The evening near'd with its arms too dense.
She laughed aloud for hours a round,
And waltzed too jocund like a bird.
Her bosoms danced yet sans a sound,
And spoke her lips no concrete word,
That thru' senses could be heard.

JOHN TYLER:

Tyler spoke in a wondrous tone,
Merry thou seem for what cause?
Is it for the azure stone?
That thou seek'st grand applause?
Hold on dear! Bite a pause.

JOHN TYLER:

'Tis just one and worth few dollars,
There's a whole ore 'neath the crust.
'Twas a lesson stolen from the scholars,

And thus I'd send thou to the dust.
And a stone so kept to befool thy trust.

JOHN TYLER:

Hither a lesson let me to thee impart,
Ne'er be happy sans a whole survey.
Be certain and triumphant in thy art,
And judge not by thy cells ain't grey.
It may plunder a sweet bright day.

JOHN TYLER:

Heart is tricky and devious a chest,
Trust not choices reared in heart.
Seek for thy mind and its behest,
And let it rein as a prudent part,
And drive thy arms thru' e'ery art.

DORA:

The woman baffled now spoke few words,
May I to the garth now hunt the ore?
And excavate 'em with my swords,
And bring those stones to thy floor?
And adorn each nook of thy shore?

JOHN TYLER:

Hold on damsel! The test is done,
And now another hunt awaits.
An agile mind ablaze as the sun,
Can only change thy wilted fates,
And open for thou those golden gates.

DORA:

O duke of ages! O knight on the crust,
Dora awaits thy stern behest.
Let thy command like a stormy gust,
Shake my visage and my queasy breasts.
Announce o Lord my ensuing test.

JOHN TYLER:

Tyler smiled. O darling! Worry not voices mine,
I yearn to train each cell in thee.
A battle awaits with a covert shine,
And there no air is sweet and free,
They're called the "Sweltering Westerly".

JOHN TYLER:

Tepid crimes and ruthless arms,
Proclaim death for whole mankind.
They ravish dames and slay off charms,
And rein the world with a demented mind.
Can we o' dear still be but a blind?

JOHN TYLER:

I've plans and stringent plans,
To stop each sinner ere they sin.
And save the world and its innocent clans,
And shower upon 'em a jocund grin.
We must win and we shalt win.

DORA:

O duke! Hither I stand by thy side forever,
And shalt fight for thou with all my might.
We shalt be like a benevolent river,
Spreading smiles thru' dreary nights,
And spreading glee with noble insights.

11. THE LAST TRIAL

<u>North Durming Island</u>

JOHN TYLER:

Hola! Arise o damsel! Behold the sun,
'Tis crimson amid the azure skies.
It's gleaming visage like a succulent bun,
Allures a million pairs of eyes,
And stands ablaze as a dawn's surprise.
Dora yawned; a couple of times,
And awoke upright to Tyler's call.
She look'd the windows and heard the chimes,
Swaying to the zephyrs of the fall,
And blush'd a while like a winsome doll.

DORA:

Where art we o noble knight?
Wherefore travel we thru' hush'd midnights?
From Lambert's lands to this eldritch site;
I feel baffled of poor insights.
Unveil to me o duke erudite.

JOHN TYLER:

Worry not damsel! Worry not thou,
North Durming is this island named.
Time is precious and so I vow
To time and honour the way 'tis sternly framed.
Nights art oft lost in sleeps untamed.

JOHN TYLER:

Days art bright to work and learn,
And test thy skills ere the final war.
Days art sweet for 'em who earn,
Warfare manoeuvres quaffing the tar,
And fight all breaths with the deepest scar.

JOHN TYLER:

This holy day hast brought thou gold,
Chances blest for a brighter sky.
Employ hours ere they're cold,
And the bleak ice age stands too nigh,
And the innocent world desires to die.

JOHN TYLER:

Behold afar! The mountains stand,
Drummers Mountain! The name they bear.

They're a good old part of the Durming land,
And grow each day with the passing air,
Miles beneath the earthen layers.

JOHN TYLER:

Somewhere there atop the tors,
A cavern awaits thee to intervene,
A sack of gold tied to a horse,
Hides amid the woodlands green.
Find it right by its godly sheen.

JOHN TYLER:

And return hither till the eve's too nigh,
And the hazel sun wilts: too frail.
Cuz nights art wolves and stars art shy,
And woods art predators in their vale,
And darkness narrates a macabre tale.

DORA:

Worry not o master! Dora fears not,
She shalt triumph each odd that stands,
And bring to thee the treasure pot,
Safe and clean from the timberlands,
And wrapp'd with courtesy; in thy hands.
Early the dawn next when the yonder skies,
Grinned pink pearls and cerulean sapphires,

And the sun smiled bright with garnet eyes,
And the world was gay in jocund attires,
Dora's dreams soar'd up and higher.
The narrow road thru' the thickset woods,
Took the damsel in twisted turns.
Big old trees with lushness stood,
And Dora walked thru' swaying ferns,
And thither she beheld few dark caverns.
The slopes were stiff with craggy tors,
Thick canopies draped 'em all.
The winds were wild and brute of course,
Discerping leaves as herald to the fall,
And frail a signal of summer's call.
Eight dark caves thither stood in pride,
Each look'd grey and bleak and dull.
Ebony skies were all inside,
Draping the woods like a vicious wall,
And Dora heard roars and a louder brawl.
She wasn't 'fraid but walked forth brave,
And stood in front of the central door.
Not door exactly but a stone engrave'd,
Yet clad in Augean sycamores,
She stood o'er a swampy floor.
Her ears were wide and mind agile,
And soul quite smart for the task bestowed.
She's walked yon miles o'er craggy piles,
Yet overcame each rutted road,
And in darkness grave her aura glowed.
She's scurrying a quest for a familiar sound,

'Twas a neigh that she's all set to hear.
A horse's moan or a cry unbound,
Was heard nowhere amid the air,
Just few frogs and a squeaking hare.
Dayspring crumbled and lay deadpan,
O'er the squelchy forest crust.
The bewitching night with its ebony clan,
Wrapp'd as duvets the winds and dust,
Dora sat still with a sky of trust.
Dreaming faeries and angels and nymphs,
The alluring night was soon at shore.
Scarlet glimpses thru' azure crimps,
Was slowly kissing the soggy floor,
And the canopies awoke with an open door.
Dora awoke with the thin sunbeams,
And the morning breeze cockled her face.
She ran amuck right off her dreams,
Thru' the yellow woods in a wilder chase,
For the horse that belongs to a regal race.
The yellow woods had lain for years,
Beyond the caves where Dora stood.
She ran for hours thru' the ebony layers,
And then beheld the yellow woods.
The caves led ways and the ways seem'd good.
A horse or a mare! Knows not she,
Yet her feet still scamper'd the woods.
She moved with the gusts of the westerly,
Oblivious of her treasured womanhood,
With gleeful a heart and a serendipitous mood.

A mile afar whence the slopes turn down,
And the woods grow frail and sparse,
And the arduous earth holds human towns,
As broken rhymes in a verse,
Dora's eyes could well behold the silhouette of a horse.
Quite as a newb she walked in hush,
And saw a horse stand bright.
Grazing the meadows green and lush,
It gleamed 'neath hazel sunlight,
And a wooden crate was just above; tied too firm and tight.
Unfeasible task though; thought the girl,
Yet her brain cells hold grey hues.
Her mind has a shine like a pinkish pearl,
And her eyes gleam like cold dews.
The horse contrary; has a brain obtuse.
Her eyes ran miles amid the woods,
They searched for a true henbane.
Hazel flowers beneath tough roods,
The plant was swaying insane.
Dora smiled for a blink or two and kiss'd her own sweet brain.
Henbane leaves she plucked a few,
Pasted 'em in a little while.
She blended 'em with a drop of dew,
Neatly extracted from the pasture pile.
Dora's mind was truly agile.
Henbane leaves into a healthy man,
Can induce the seeds of aeonian slumber.
And for hours the sun seems wan,
And the stars appear as a countable number.

Henbane makes each arm encumber.
The cakes so drenched in henbane drops,
Were hurled with care into the leas.
The grazing horse with the moorland crops,
Chew'd the cakes with gleeful ease.
And yawn'd quite wide to the wafting breeze.
And little a while as time pass'd by,
The horse was snoring still and quite.
Dora unlaced the crate with a sigh,
And pull'd it down with all her might,
And dragged it till the eve grinned bright.
A nook she found amid the cave,
Little stones were scattered around.
Her mellow'd arms were stout and brave,
And enkindl'd fire on the ground.
She burned the arid foliage mound.
A lone long night as she slept in peace,
And dreamt good love she made erstwhile.
All so sudden she heard a hiss,
From beneath some archaic skeleton piles,
That'd lain since ages in this isle.
'Twas a black mamba! Deadly to the core,
With ireful fangs and confluent eyes,
It gazed yet higher from the cavern's floor,
And gazed too sharp as a grim surprise.
Dora stayed calm and play'd too wise.
A little stick that lay at a nook,
Served her recourse and another chance,
The flame that danced as a foaming brook,

Took the serpent's sudden glance,
And Dora had an austere countenance.
A little fire she borrowed thence,
And held the stick firm upright.
The unnerved serpent missed a sense,
And tacitly scurried into the night,
Dora stood with a frail insight.
Hours hence when the skies turn'd blue,
The appalling night was off yon bays.
Dora dragged the crate anew,
And pranced back town thru' the same old ways,
Leaving behind two swaggering days.

12. THE GAME PLAN

<u>*South Hampshire*</u>

Oft thru' the streets of South Hampshire,
A strange couple was seen by many.
Clad in weird and eldritch attires,
They mimed as paupers with no penny,
Is it real or a grand irony?
Gladiator's Avenue; Thomson enclave,
Flat two not four; second floor.
Secretly a voice whispered; a slave,
A slave from the thievish store,
Bring me right at my door.
A silhouette disappeared into the dark,
The old man perched by the porch alone.
The night sky look'd too bare and stark,
And a frail voice and a feeble moan,
Shook the walls with a beseeching tone.

STRANGE OLD MAN:

Wherefore art thou 'fraid o girl?
The diamond or and the crate of gold.
Dost thou not remember? Thou art a pearl,

Pink and worthy! Calm and cold,
And priceless a gem ne'er to be sold.

STRANGE OLD MAN:

There's chaos in thy buried soul,
And voices many speak to thee.
Thou art brave! Behold thy goal,
'Tis noble and wise and blemishes free,
Trust thy heart if not me.

DORA:

O duke! Wherefore bide we in disguise?
An old man thou and a granny for me.
Wherefore a slave for a hefty price?
And who's that silhouette? Unveil to me,
I feel oft drowned in an ebony sea.

DORA:

All tasks I did and hurdles I leaped,
And brought thou gold and diamonds; right?
From Lambert's and Durmings; ne'er I heaved,
But spent grim hours in the arms of the nights,
In dark bleak caves sans a tinge of light.

DORA:

Ne'er yet to my yearning ears,
Thou hast poured the truth that's true.
And noble goals that o'er the years
Thou said; art still to me fresh and new,
Am I thy slave or a real beau?

STRANGE OLD MAN:

(JOHN TYLER)

O damsel! O dulcinea of my fancy thoughts,
Wherefore baffled thou on this day?
Thou art an amorous gift I bought,
Thou art the protagonist of my play,
Think not much! No more words thou say.

JOHN TYLER:

I shalt map the schemes and plans,
And reveal each word to thy snoopy mind.
We shalt hire more men to the clan,
And they must all be good and kind,
And in days a few; 'em we shalt find.

JOHN TYLER:

Patience o dear! Let's not fall a trench,
This house seems safe with a secret door.

And all thy thirst this duke shalt quench,
And shalt feed thou noesis evermore,
Till we conquer each desolate shore.

JOHN TYLER:

I'd but always all my life,
Hated crimes and sinners a lot.
To prune their roots with the sharpest knife,
Reined the realm of my noble thoughts.
'Tis no cypher or an otiose nought.

JOHN TYLER:

Where cops stand dull and sans a speech,
And sinful brutes art safe and free.
This duke; o dear to the Lords beseech,
For power and strength to cut each tree,
That bears the fruits of a devious spree.

JOHN TYLER:

The man who ravishes women each day,
And slays 'em off with a brutal soul.
Yet no evidence claims a say,
And he's too prudent in his goal,
What purgatory o'er him shalt from heavens fall?
Dora's eyes were flames and fires,
Her fingers clasped to Tyler's hand.

He felt her outburst hued in ire,
And a strong desire to reprimand,
And slay those men on every land.

JOHN TYLER:

This flame we need and let it burn,
O dear girl; too brave art thou.
I've good faith that thou shalt learn,
And for a blest world; take a vow,
And start thy work from the moment now.

JOHN TYLER:

I tested thy skills and thy true mind frame,
The first two tasks were trials for thee.
I'm well convinced for the deadly game,
Thou shalt triumph each day in glee,
And let each sinner be purged and free.

JOHN TYLER:

Let each chaos that bides inside,
Embrace slumber in covert graves.
Hear thy voice and it shalt guide,
To prance in pride thru' the world of knaves,
And slay off brute each Satan's slave.

JOHN TYLER:

The night's too dark and the moon's nowhere,
Ghastly winds art ruffling past.
Sleep o girl and let me care,
And shade thy soul from evil's dust,
And plant thou strong on the heaven's crust.
The dayspring shower'd glorious glances,
Of hazel rains from the cerulean skies.
The bustling city in happy chances,
Danced with a million gleeful eyes,
And feted amour in a bleak disguise.
Dora awoke to the first daybreak,
The warm sunlight was all on fields.
The squeaking birds by the Houston Lake;
Were gleaming hazel; as a metal shield,
And waltzing gay to the floral yields.
There's a map and a plan to run,
And arms were all scattered around.
The disguised Tyler 'neath the sun,
Was busy decoding eldritch sounds,
And coloured papers were flying unbound.

DORA:

Good Morning Duke! Quoth a voice,
Sweeter than the buzzing bees.
And sonorous as a chime of choice,
As a psithurism by the woodland trees,

Or a soft wave thru' abysmal seas.

JOHN TYLER:

Good Morning love! How good art dreams?
Those art pure when a man's awake.
And serve 'em goals as a repeating glimpse.
The slumberous dreams art oft too fake,
As fruits of a rhythmic junk intake.

JOHN TYLER:

Purge thy mind and purge thy soul,
Breathe in the zephyrs of the scarlet morn.
Perch beneath the sunshine whole,
And let thy thoughts themselves adorn,
With the beaut of ages as they're born.

JOHN TYLER:

Hither o dear come and nestle at ease,
Hear'st thou all I've to say.
Behold the map! Hold it; let it not sway to the breeze,
Else we shalt be punished at the last doomsday,
Tasks all in sequence are marked in grey.

JOHN TYLER:

Three miles east is a land of shops,

Boisterous crowd there reins each hour.
Little a power of the puppet cops,
They stand afar as wilted flowers,
Or hide aghast behind tall bowers.

JOHN TYLER:

Thither awaits a coquettish churl,
Dealing gold and gems all blue.
Too lustful a man for voluptuous girls,
And sip each damsel like cold dew,
Ere they perceive a tinge of clue.

JOHN TYLER:

Adept is he to con each man,
And befool a crowd of gullible souls.
There's few more to his evil clan,
They all hold bright a perfect goal,
And hide in cloaks of an innocent mole.

JOHN TYLER:

For years he's sly yet prances roads,
And brags to men his spurious name.
He's David Brown and writes fake odes,
And savours a lot his knavish game,
And fetes each day his gaudy fame.

JOHN TYLER:

We must thither in adroit disguise,
Paint great images as a true meathead.
Let all men; those argute and wise,
Pity us both with compassion instead,
Our roles art effortful thus cagily be play'd.

JOHN TYLER:

The days that follow must offer to us,
Triumphant medals of glistening gold.
Brown's soul shalt breathe good cuss,
And his treasures will ne'er be sold,
But lie 'neath bare dust; bleak and cold.

13. THE LAST CONFESSION

Dales Brook Town

The train was time and right with hours,
Santiago remain'd miles behind.
Tyler bought some perfumed flowers,
And walk'd up straight with a stable mind,
As a truthful part of humankind.
And for a moment he did recall,
Artist Jerry and his smiling face.
Memories grave like a scary doll,
Haunted him with cold disgrace.
Yet he walk'd firm thru' the race.
He recall'd a moment the old cop then,
Ran amuck behind him days.
And knavish his demeanour befooled good men,
And scattered around grim disgrace.
And triumph'd in e'ery sinful race.
No doubts remain his purpose hailed,
And served good causes e'ery time.
Facinorous souls were lashed and jailed,
And punished well for their crimes,

As 'tis done by digestive enzymes.
The roads were still bit similar though,
Changes occured in faces around.
Novice visages with time did grow,
And old ones sank 'neath hours profound,
The world each day is growing unbound.
Quite nigh before him; stood,
The same old cop shop as eons ere.
The rusted gate with an iron hood,
Holds new names o'er its layer,
With time there comes a change in share.
Tyler pushed it open and wide,
And walk'd timidly thru' the door.
A cop sat lone and none inside,
And bygone dust; were all on floor.
He heard him lavishly sit and snore.
A little knock on the wooden door,
And the cop was high on both his feet.
He gazed at Tyler for seconds score,
And gestured him to have a seat,
And asked him whom he wants to meet?

JOHN TYLER:

Tyler quoth then coy and meek,
With timid a voice too muffled to hear.
"Lend me a minute to settle and speak,
And I shalt make my statements clear."
Tyler wiped his gushing tears.

JOHN TYLER:

Where art all thy senior men?
The sergeant is now all I seek.
I gotta make a confession,
And let me speak ere my heart turns weak,
And my voice lone defies to speak.

WALT STEVENS:

Wait a minute Mr? What's thy name?
I am the trooper and thou might say.
The sergeant is off for a baseball game,
And might return by the end of day,
And that too dubious; I said he may.
Tyler pondered for minutes whole two,
And began his tale with all his grit.
One aft one with pellucid clue,
He quoth all words with no more wit,
Every word; bit by bit as he deemed fit.
For one whole hour his voice didn't stop,
And poor the trooper was ensorcelled right.
His aweary ears as wilted crops,
Heard each word and felt each plight,
And fancied each sequence clean and bright.
After hours of an absorbing story,
The trooper quoth his words at last.

WALT STEVENS:

(SON OF THE SERGEANT MARC STEVENS)

Hail o writer; long live thy glory,
How prudently as a tempest gust,
Narrated thou these tales of past.

WALT STEVENS:

Agile a writer indeed art thou,
Publish it for wealth and fame.
Let me stand and let me vow,
This tale's better than the baseball game,
And better than this real mayhem.

JOHN TYLER:

Excuse me Sir, this isn't a tale,
But my truth; the blunt truth quoth I.
I've slay'd good men by the northern dale,
And seen 'em heave and wilt to die.
I've seen their corpses deadpan lie.

JOHN TYLER:

Sinful I am; facinorous a soul,
And all I have is sheer remorse.

Push me behind those little holes,
And lash me hard with all thy force,
I seek punishment; give me worse.
The trooper laughed and then arose,
And clapped a couple of times aloud.

WALT STEVENS:

Thou art perfect, nearly close,
Thou gonna make us really proud,
And hither I'm entirely wowed.

WALT STEVENS:

A writer and an actor too,
So well play'd as 'twas no reel,
But thy truth, it seem'd so true,
And gave me a gust of a real feel,
Of distorted mind and a demonic zeal.

WALT STEVENS:

But perhaps thou art wrongly destined,
'Tis a cop shop and not a press.
Go back and now with a pellucid mind,
Shed off worries and otiose stress,
And give thy thoughts a worthy dress.
Tyler tried a few times more,
But all his yearnings called in vain.

He walk'd out thence thru' the wooden door,
And filled his cheeks in remorseful rain.
He felt a tinge of harrowing pain.
In a garth nigh to the cop shop place,
Two cops strolled and chaffer'd at ease.
"I feel bad when I behold his face,
Overly pale like wilted trees,
Impassive e'en to the sweetest breeze."

CONVERSATION BETWEEN TWO POLICEMEN:

True thou feel'st and so do I,
Marc Stevens was a gallant man.
He lost his mind to an offender sly,
And landed amid the asylum clan,
A brute he's who broke this man.
Poor his son aft days of mourning,
Return'd again to his college gates.
He liv'd yet stronger e'ery morning,
And gleefully reconcil'd to his fates,
And spent his days sans human mates.
He quoth no word nor voiced his pain,
All day long with books he fought.
With passing hours he brimm'd his brain,
With knowledge more and sapient thoughts,
And moulded himself; as a utile pot.
Soon aft years he joined the force,
Though as a trooper; he's sure to rise.
And one fine day with the best of a source,

He shalt touch the azure skies,
And we shalt savour it with our eyes.
Walt Stevens a day shalt rein,
Whole a clan of able men.
And e'ery battle this lad must win,
With guns and swords and a tinselled pen.
And we shalt witness brave Marc again.
Tyler felt a thousand volts,
Scurrying amuck thru' his fragile bones.
And all so deadly thunderbolts,
Made him yell with a burst of groans.
He felt a jet of pelted stones.
He rushed inside heaving fast,
And right in front of Walt he stood.
He wept too frantic with stings of past,
And dire bites of his bleak childhood,
He stood in hush as a lifeless wood.

WALT STEVENS:

Hey! Wherefore return'st thou hither again?
Leave I said; great a man art thou.
What wealth thou seek'st or what good gain?
No purpose shalt thee gain'st now,
Leave I said; great man art thou.
Walt's words were clamorous though,
They soothed the wounds in Tyler's heart.
But there's more story that he must know,
Ere thence he forever departs,

Boarding to heaven the final cart.

JOHN TYLER:

Wherefore thou forgiv'st me?
Thou art aware of the sins I made.
I'm too evil; a venomous tree,
Awaiting blows of a deadly blade,
And sleep fore'er in my tomb instead.

WALT STEVENS:

Walt smiled! Nay; smirk'd for a while,
Sit; quoth he, still mild and meek.
I'll take thou behind few mysterious miles,
Hear'st me calm; feel'st not weak.
Thou at times might feel'st too bleak.

WALT STEVENS:

A decade behind I'll escort thee,
Marc Stevens then reined quite brave.
His stern bravery foamed like a sea,
And frightened the corpses laid 'neath graves,
And frightened the criminals like dumb slaves.

WALT STEVENS:

One fine day he came home dim,

And quoth no word the whole day long.
And by the night I heard him scream,
And sing quite loud an eldritch song,
With their lyrics; obscene and wrong.

WALT STEVENS:

I went to him and sought an answer,
But he kept dancing highs and lows.
He look'd alike a lunatic dancer,
Or a man with strong drug dose.
Soon he fell on the floor; comatose.

WALT STEVENS:

Years later an evening came,
And we were there in the asylum's garth.
Dad was good and play'd good games,
And savoured his life close to the earth,
He spoke that eve a tale of worth.

WALT STEVENS:

All these time we blamed thee; John,
And never forgave thy brute slyness.
But that very eve by the fountain lawn,
Our thoughts were given a different dress,
Made of respect, honour and grace.

WALT STEVENS:

He quoth to us his own mistake,
Ere a cop he's a human being.
And what all happened by the northern lake,
Broke my dad's treasur'd wings,
And filled his soul with remorseful stings.

WALT STEVENS:

He got to learn thy purpose then,
And he burned himself in grave lament.
He wrote verses back in den,
And always wrote; thou art God sent,
To mend humanity and repair each dent.

WALT STEVENS:

He always thought in lone dark rooms,
One bullet hath ta'en thy soul.
Though thy ways were dark as fumes,
Yet thy purpose had a nobler goal.
'Twas not a sin or a deed that's fowl.

WALT STEVENS:

Always taught he his sagacious words,
And quaff'd 'em I as a nostrum pure.
And thus today I use my swords,

To help weak ones from brute censure,
And end all crimes as an eternal cure.

WALT STEVENS:

Thou ain't sinful o dear: John,
Return in pride and triumph more races.
Serve this world in thy ways alone,
And paint more smiles on despondent faces,
And rescue 'em from grim disgraces.

WALT STEVENS:

Thy place is thither in the open world,
Pour the honey that bides in thee.
The earth is still too bleak and cold,
And men are still in chains; unfree.
Heal their wounds; shower good glee.

WALT STEVENS:

The world needs more such men as thee,
And I too wanna be a part.
Aid me always like the oldest tree,
And as a hermit drive my cart,
O Tyler; thou must ne'er depart.

WALT STEVENS:

I always felt thou still art alive,
Death is yonder still for thee.
There's a cosmos for thou to drive,
And break more shackles and set 'em free,
And pour good zephyrs as a divine tree.

WALT STEVENS:

We be mates and mates evermore,
Note my digits and make calls rife.
Flourish more in Santiago's shore,
And fete thy days of a blissful life,
With thy children and sweet wife.

JOHN TYLER:

Tyler gazed at him too awed,
How come so much know'st thee?
I've not said a single word;
Do thou read'st minds and spree?
Like that hermit 'neath the tree?

WALT STEVENS:

I'm no recluse O rever'd man,
Spoke good Walt in a serene voice.
I am a cop and thus my clan,
Gets me wisdom of my choice,
That too tacitly sans much noise.

WALT STEVENS:

I play'd a bit with thy foaming mind,
I knew thou must to me return.
Thou art truthful to mankind,
For, in remorse thy heart did burn,
Though much wealth thy skills hath earn'd.

WALT STEVENS:

But one a doubt I still feel more,
What hath caused thee; grave remorse?
Punishing criminals soothes thy core,
And 'tis blissful I feel; of course.
Then why dost thou feel so worse?

JOHN TYLER:

Tyler feebly smiled a bit,
Walt; serving mankind has more great ways.
Ere my soul was not well lit,
Thus I slay'd more men for days,
To punish a criminal aft my chase.

JOHN TYLER:

But when the rose of love did bloom,
And drenched me in its aroma whole.

I found inside a different room,
Where bides my second soul,
Whose thoughts are chaste like a tinselled bowl.

JOHN TYLER:

E'ery human that carries a life,
Carries inside two polar souls.
One sleeps hushed and one speaks rife,
And one at a time their mind; controls,
And drives all roads in varied roles.

JOHN TYLER:

Love and hatred both art free,
And waft in winds around each one.
Either one as a magic tree,
Moulds the thoughts as the yonder sun,
And thus so different art humans.

JOHN TYLER:

The ones who grow with hatred winds,
Grow up wild and brute a day.
And cause on earth some massive ruins,
And to humans cause dismay.
Their souls art bleak, cold and grey.

JOHN TYLER:

And if perchance an amorous drop,
Rears his seeds deep inside.
He shalt reap all verdant crops,
Of kindness that shalt ne'er hide,
And ne'er forsake him like a tide.

JOHN TYLER:

Transformed a man now I've been,
And so shalt be till arms of death.
Much of the world I too have seen,
Varied races and varied faith,
But all have a common blood and breath.

JOHN TYLER:

Nothing more with murders I swear,
All for goodness I shalt live.
Helping people engrossed in fear,
Is truly divine; I believe,
And so their dreams I shalt thus weave.

JOHN TYLER:

And so for the day do grant me adieu,
Gonna travel I; off long miles to the west.
Note my address with a heart anew.

I know our bond be the best,
And thus must call for a grandeur fest.
Walt beheld with snuffling eyes,
The wheels of the train rolled off.
A reflection of the azure skies,
Fell oblique to the cop shop,
With a silhouette of a dead cop.
Promises nestled in his solitary mind,
And dreams were weaved o'er night.
For, a life to serve this humankind,
Might call for wars to fight,
But that must heal their plight.
The world is strange and so art men,
Friends and foes art crude man-made.
A friend this day might still but cozen,
And allure one to a sinful trade,
And stab quite oft for penny and bread.
Once a foe might soothe for a life,
And protect us from trenches dark.
They might guide us well too rife,
And midst lone roads give a glowing spark,
And aid us fruitful in our work.
Time is Lord, who plays all day,
With relations, bonds and work and age.
'Tis a game and we must play,
With patience and wit like a sapient sage,
To get imprinted on a clinquant page.

14. FATE'S PRESSIE

<u>*Santiago Islands*</u>

The aurora smiled with a gleeful grin,
The scarlet streaks were all thru' the skies.
Dora awoke by five to win,
The favour of the dawn that kisses her eyes.
The bliss of the dawn is a blest surprise.
A sudden gust of the cold north winds,
Ruffling thru' the light of the glorious dawn,
Gave her memories of the wilful ruins,
And made her yearn and mourn for John,
She wept secretly all alone.
Zeus was still asleep in dreams,
Alex by the next room slept in bliss.
Dora walk'd down amid blest sunbeams,
And savoured again; the crimson kiss.
She pray'd to the skies to grant her wish.
The sea was foaming with the morning tides,
The shore was not so crowded still.
The sun was gayly gleaming in pride,
From behind the northern hills,
As a part of its quite a cadenced drill.
Too sudden a glimpse and Dora gazed awed,

Tyler prance'd with a jocund face.
She stood a stone as a glimpse of God,
And cherished the moment; of utmost grace.
As if she triumph'd a hard-fought race.
The two love birds; too wild and blue,
Rushed as a gust into each one.
Their arms clenched firm and thus the two,
Savoured the morning beneath the sun,
As bodies two but the soul as one.
They walk'd back home grinning too wide,
Delightful were their visages bright.
Tyler's desires foamed inside,
And waited he keen for the solitary night,
To make good love with lustful delight.
They chaffer'd o'er the morning beverage,
Tyler told her all that's true.
That fate was great and now as a sage,
Guided him on paths anew,
To serve mankind beneath the blue.
He narrated whole the rendezvous,
'Tween him and Walt, the heir of Marc.
He quoth all that he learned anew,
And thus as a flame amid the dark,
He found a mate as fate's remark.
He quoth his plans to serve mankind,
With Alex and Walt on journeys new.
Dora may hire new maids to mind,
The burritos store and her household too.
And he shalt be a social crew.

Dora's eyes were smudged and wet,
Emotions foamed within her soul.

DORA:

Dear love; 'tis not thy fate,
Thou mistook thy divine goal,
And misconstrued the godly call.

DORA:

Stay back hither and aid me feed,
And serve those men in need of care.
Gratuitous 'tis to find frail seeds,
Forsaking the wretched ones in bleak air,
Hanging hopeless for their share.

DORA:

Look around; hear 'em cry; bleak outcry,
Plunder'd by fate and ruined by time.
They too have the same cerulean sky,
But lands have changed in arms of crime,
And sway to 'em as broken chimes.

DORA:

They find boulders in roads they tread,
And hunger gnaws 'em long all day.

And crust to 'em is a thorn of dread,
And the ivory moon seems bleak and grey.
Serv'st 'em thou; hear'st 'em say.
Tyler's eyes were awash in brine,
Tears walk'd down his freckled cheeks.
He beheld afar thru' the yonder vines,
And a man lone perching; frail for weeks,
Caught his glances; like a click.

JOHN TYLER:

Who's he? Enquir'd he in a trembling voice,
A thousand falcons gnaw'd his soul.
He heard outcries; a terrible noise,
Like clamorous howls from earthen holes,
And noises raucous as breaking bowls.

DORA:

He's Mr Alfred; homeless a man,
For days I've seen him on this shore,
Oft adrift; he hath years ere he lost his clan,
And lost all wealth and doors and floors.
He lives by the fern vine; starving of course.

DORA:

Sometimes out of humane a heart,
I've fed him from the little I hold.

He'd always wanted and yearned to depart,
But my humanity is yet not sold,
And my heart hath not slept meh and cold.

JOHN TYLER:

Why haven't thou to the castle brought?
Our castle is big with rooms galore.
The old man must to cold get caught,
And freeze to death on the frozen shore.
Bring him in; I'll open the door.

DORA:

Dora smirk'd; what think'st thou sweetie?
I've had implor'd him hours and days.
I beseech'd him to leave cloths dirty,
And accept gayly our warm embrace,
But he says nothing but a pale brown face.

JOHN TYLER:

Let me try and I trust God,
The old man must to me respond.
I shalt house him in our abode,
And with him weave a cordial bond,
Bak'st thou cookies with grilled almonds.
Tyler walk'd thru' the swathes of sands,
Old Alfred was weak and pale.

He perched in hush with wizened hands,
And a countenance too swooning and frail,
As if aweary from a prolonged sail.

JOHN TYLER:

Hola Mr Alfred; whence art thee?
Wherefore thou on this barren heath?
And solitary 'neath this redwood tree,
How more blissful can thou breathe?
Thither's all wild ferns and hemlock weeds.

JOHN TYLER:

Behold hither; I'm named John Tyler,
Christened by my rever'd mom.
I own a sacred Christian smiler,
Yet lived thru' harshness bleak in form,
A treacherous father and a cruddy dorm.

JOHN TYLER:

I've earn'd good wealth and a little renown,
All by choices and ne'er by fate.
I've ploughed for days in barren towns,
Yet found no man who claim'd a mate,
And closed on face their tinselled gates.

JOHN TYLER:

A wasted childhood and shattered youth,
And if at all I've dreamt few times,
They were all macabre and that was sooth,
Songs were all like broken chimes,
Or distorted verses with no rhymes.
Mr Alfred arose and gazed,
Gazed at Tyler; quiet and lone,
His eyes were for a moment amazed,
They look'd so like a shining stone,
Shimmering on a regal throne.
His ivory hairs to the zephyrs sway'd,
And a little smile adorned his face.
The frowns vanished and happiness play'd,
Its jocund roles in varied ways.
He raised an arm and bestowed grace.

JOHN TYLER:

And thus I beseech to thee with truth,
Comest thou inside my house.
I shalt serve thee with all my youth,
And so shalt do my beloved spouse.
Thou devour all meals and get a good drowse.

JOHN TYLER:

Trust me! I'm lot like thy beloved child,

And thus shalt serve thee; rest of days.
With love and bliss and gestures mild,
I shalt cater thee in all good ways.
And protect thee off all bleak dismays.
Mr Alfred look'd stonking soon,
And a little smile was all his face.
In a frail voice with a touch of boon,
Muttered he; gemulitch in Tyler's grace,
And raised his trembling arms to embrace.
And thus for years the 'Tylers' grew,
And served good men; in hapless plights.
Their store ran miles and kiss'd yon blue,
And reach'd with years greater heights,
And Tyler savoured his blissful nights.
Alex came miles and still is strong,
Dora's all worthy to drive the cart.
Tyler's life is a sweet old song,
Dulcet to his youthful heart.
And that has become his closest part.
A thousand hapless people each day,
And orphans and all helpless those,
Hails his name and words they say,
"All for John our spirits arose,
'Tis his grace the Lord God knows".
Twice a hundred acres of land,
And four new outlets; regal and bright,
The Gyron's Haven was a noble brand,
Gleaming e'en at dark midnights,
And triumphing each day; more maiden heights.

About The Author

Dipanjan Bhattacharjee (Author, Poet and Engineer)

Dipanjan Bhattacharjee is an engineer by profession and a writer by passion. He hails from the state of Jharkhand in India. He has completed his B.Tech in ELECTRONICS AND INSTRUMENTATION Engineering in 2016. He has been into literature since his school days. To be specific he first explored his abilities when he was in his seventh standard. Writing simultaneously in 3 languages namely English, Bengali and Hindi makes him stand out of the crowd. He has recieved a myriad of laurels till date. He has had achieved over a 1000 certificates from various national and international literary communities and also has received titles like Literary Colonel by Story Mirror and nominations for International Book Of Records for Longest Poem and Palindromic Poem. Recently, he has been felicitated with the Next Generation Writer Award for the year 2021 from NAZMEHAYAT. His other achievements include being nominated as the Author of the Week a several times by Story mirror and consecutive winner in Nazme Hayat. He has been conferred with Poet of the Month from an international writers forum Realm of Poems for the month of February, 2021. He has been conferred with Poetry Celebrity Award, ADVANCE DIPLOMA IN POETRY AND A GRADUATE DIPLOMA IN POETRY from Sri Lanka. He also has been conferred with Medallion De Honor from French Poetic Society. He has been selected winner for writing a poetry on Sustaining Wildlife put forth by UN. Currently he is also serving as The Regional Manager of Asia Division in one of the International Writer's Community based in Sri Lanka. He is an expert in 30 plus International Poetry Forms till date and has also authored several solo books on poetry, short stories and a novel. He has also co authored in several best selling anthologies and that too in all three languages. He has also compiled a handful of anthologies.

He has been featured in national and international literary journals such as Chrysanthemum Chronicles, Bharat Vision(Amazon Best Seller) and also has been featured in a national magazine Tare Zameen Par. His hobbies include listening to music especially classical and thumri. Also long drive and photography fills him with immense joy. Being a poet he has many gurus and favourite poets namely William Shakespeare, William Wordsworth, John Keats, P.B Shelley, Byron and Robert Frost in English Language, Rabindranath Tagore, Sukanta Bhattacharjee, Kaji Nazru Islam and Michel Madhusudan Dutta in Bengali language.

Some of his books are namely;

1. Cosmos of Tranquillity (140 Poems)

2. Corsage of Cadences (150 Poems)

3. Voice of Youth: A Step Against Rape

4. Twinkling Souls

5. Womb: A Journey into Motherhood

6. Hauntings of The Hilly Hamlet (Novel)

7. Idyllic Poesies (50 Poems)

8. The Sorted Six (6 Short Stories)

9. Reveries: An Array of Verses

Other than poetry he also has many research papers in various science journals about cognitive neuroscience, brain imaging, brain mapping, artificial intelligence, machine learning and other myriad dimensions.

Overall, he is very interesting to explore and befriend. Often named as the wonder guy or prodigy, he is very down to earth and loves to learn about different languages, nations and communities.